Everybody On,
Nobody Out

Everybody On, Nobody Out

Hope and possibility in the New York Collegiate Baseball League

Paul Casey Gotham

For Dad,

Who introduced me to the virtues of the game.

Contents

Chapter 1
Opening Day

Forecasters called for ninety degrees, and the sun was doing everything it could to make the meteorologists look good. The Summer Solstice wouldn't actually occur for another two weeks, but this afternoon of June seventh could easily pass for the dog days of July or August. Waves of heat lifted from the grass. Only the cicadas or locusts, whose rhythmic hum augments the rays of the sun, were missing.

Gone were the windbreakers and long-sleeve under-garments worn by the players two days previous at the team's first practice. One comes to expect such drastic temperature shifts in this region where the term lake effect is a part of everyday conversations. The slightest shift in wind direction can easily cause a fifteen degree fluctuation in the mercury.

The loud speakers of the Clark V. Whited Baseball Complex squawk with a jukebox of tunes. It is almost as if the songs are being played from an LP record; the speakers have their own snap, crackle and pop. While Mick Jagger finishes crooning his "Midnight Rambler," and Keith Richards's last guitar chord rings, the snap of leather into horsehide can be heard as baseballs get tossed here and there. The crack of a wood bat sounds from the batting cage. Today is Opening Day for the 2007 New York Collegiate Baseball League (NYCBL) season. The Brockport Riverbats host the Webster Yankees on the campus of The State University of New York at Brockport.

Young men clad in their pinstriped uniforms dot the field. Gary Helmick, Ryan Sullivan, Nelson Santos and Rob Lawler are the last to get in batting practice. The infielders rotate through six hacks at a time and trot out of the cage while the next in line jogs to and takes his place on the tarp placed over the batter's box area.

Joe McIntyre and Marcus Nidiffer, or "KB" as he will become known, scoop balls on the infield. Josh Johnson, Jason Stifler, Mark Stuckless, Josh Brown, Bryan Gardner and Jacob Bernath shag flies in the outfield while their Webster Yankee teammates finish "BP."

Eugene Offerman tends to the bucket. He positions himself behind the protective fence placed ten yards off second base on the outfield grass. As the outfielders retrieve hit balls, they toss them to the Curacao native, and he places the "pearls" in a canvas bag. Gino's choice of roles is no coincidence. Pitchers, save for the day's starting pitcher, share the vital role of bucket man. Gino, being the lone returning starter, recognizes the stability he can provide and the example he can set. When beckoned, Gino grabs the handle made of heavy rope and breaks into full stride. He understands the value of time during batting practice. He also understands that as a returning player he needs to set an example for others to follow.

On a raised platform placed between the mound and home plate stands Mike Kelly. The young head coach calmly goes through the paces of delivering batting practice from behind an L-screen. At thirty, Kelly has managed to maintain his boyish good looks, and one wouldn't be surprised if the coach still needed to provide proof of age when purchasing adult beverages. Despite his age, Kelly possesses incomparable poise. He continues through this exercise with nary a flinch as the L-screen deflects line drives just inches away. It is easy to recognize the comfort Mike Kelly feels within his own skin. If self-assurance is the singular quality of a man, Kelly possesses it.

Kelly is an iconoclast of sorts. He does not seek to overthrow popular ideas as an act of random defiance. No, Kelly stands apart because he is himself. In an age where tanning beds have grown from a cottage industry into a perceived necessity, and where surgeons prostitute themselves on billboards advertising for lunchtime liposuction, Mike Kelly stands apart from the group because he accepts who he is.

This self-assurance extends beyond Mike Kelly's physical appearance and is on display the following night when the Webster Yankees travel to play the Niagara Falls Power.

***

There at Sal Maglie Field (named for the former major leaguer born and raised in this western New York city) Kelly's team experiences an early-season meltdown. Starting pitcher, Blair Veenema danced through mine fields in the first two innings before striking out the first two batters of the third. Then there is a hot smash up the middle. A dying quail falls into right field. The field umpire misses a call at first, and the Power bats around the order. Before reliever Chris Coleman records the final out, Niagara plates eight runners.

Two innings later, six more runs and another relief pitcher later, Kelly lets out a horse sigh and retreats from the top step of the dugout to take a seat on the bench. The picture has a Rockwellian air about it: the young coach, chin in hand, staring out at a carnage of sorts with his starting pitcher slumped next to him. If ever a picture were needed for the margin of a dictionary page to illustrate the definition of the word beleaguered, Kelly and Veenema have provided it.

One out from retiring the side in the third inning, Veenema takes the loss after giving up eight runs in the stanza. As he exits the mound, the loud speakers serenade him with Daniel Powter's "Bad Day."

It is at this point early in the season when a young team can begin to take on its personality. There is a tangible tension in the air. An ominous silence hangs over the dugout. Fourteen to zero can kill the spirit of any young team.

4

The construction of Sal Maglie field allows for conversations from the fans to be heard in the dugout. With the dugout built into the ground, fans in the first row of the bleachers can rest their feet upon its roof, and the aluminum roof allows for the passage of sound waves. It is at this point, with Kelly and Veenema sitting perfectly still staring out at the field when a young fan can be overheard quietly speaking to his father: "Gee dad, these Yankees really suck!"

At this moment, Kelly lifts his head and glances at his starting pitcher. The two make eye contact, share a smile and burst into laughter. Kelly continues laughing as he bounces back to the top step of the dugout. His team will go on to score five runs before its final out. The amount will not be enough for a win, but it will be enough to lift their spirits. Later Kelly summed it up: "That was one game in a forty-two game schedule; we're not going to dwell on that one too long."

...As Webster finishes batting practice in anticipation of Opening Day's first pitch, the Riverbats file back onto the field. In a routine that will take place before every game, players of the home team perform the grounds keeping. These college players aspire to earn a spot on a Major League roster. Rosters filled with players accustomed to the pampering entitled to monarchy. Yet here in the NYCBL, there is no such pampering.

Smiles and grins wiped across the faces of these young men show the kinship shared as they prepare the field for battle. Though most will only call the field at

SUNY Brockport their home for two months, today, it is their diamond. This is not the mundane task of mowing the lawn of their parents' yards. This field, this diamond, represents their sanctuary.

Three players join together and drag the batting cage, or "turtle," down the left field line and out of play. One grabs the molded handle and pulls the apparatus which is fitted with a pair of casters for portability. Teammates stand on opposite sides and push the cage.

The infield needs manicuring. Two players grab landscaping rakes. With a wide head filled with short, blunt teeth, the tools allow the players a wide area of coverage. One player grooms the area around first base while another works at third, careful to smooth any possible divot that might cause an awkward bounce.

Two more players head to the pitcher's mound, one with a deep-tooth garden rake and another with a tamper. The mound needs smoothing and leveling before today's hurlers mark their own areas for a plant foot.

Down the right field line, catcher, Adam Perlo, is in the bullpen warming up today's starter, Bryan Pullyblank.

Meanwhile, a group of Yankees gather off the field. Brown, Coleman, Bernath, Johnson, Lawler and Bobby DiNuzzo join in a game of "two-ball." Standing in a circle facing each other one player takes two balls and tosses them in any direction. Like a game of hot potato the players attempt to keep the balls moving without dropping any. The players refer to the activity's ability to develop hand-to-eye coordination.

The activity draws the ire of assistant coach, Dave Brust, who compares it to hacky-sack.

"I don't have a problem with hacky sack, but it is something you do with a beer in hand; not when you're preparing for a baseball game. You wanna develop hand-to-eye for a baseball game? Play pepper! That's hand-to-eye!"

Brust spent three years playing minor league baseball in the Atlanta Braves' organization. His sturdy build reflects the years of working on the diamond.

Field preparations continue.

Some players grab a fire hose and spray down the dirt. Five players in a line carry the hose draped over the shoulders, careful to not let it drag on the in-field grass for fear of damaging the lush, green carpet.

Others busy themselves laying down the first base line. One player grabs the chalker from the storage shed. Like a lawn fertilizer, the canister is a three-gallon steel container balanced on four wheels. The difference is that instead of dispensing dust in orbital fashion, the chalker creates the clearly defined three inches of white powder from the batter's box to first base. Another "Bat" grabs a bag of chalk, using a pair of scissors cuts it open and carefully empties the bag into the canister.

Two players extend a piece of twine from the corner of home plate to first base and carefully set the line with a pair of stakes. Two more "Bats" attend to the batter's box. They position a wooden frame around home plate. Powdered chalk is sprinkled using a cylindrical, plastic potato chip container. Holes are drilled in the twist-off top like a salt shaker. The container is filled with the white powder, and a Brockport player carefully works the dust around the inside of the frame. For the final touches field-marking paint in spray cans is used to doll up the base bags and home plate.

Among the group of Riverbats is shortstop, Jacob Kaase(Kah-say). The native of Austin, Texas will go three for four on the afternoon with a double, three runs batted in and a run scored. The shortstop plays an integral part of three double plays turned by the Brockport infield. Two inning-ending double plays occur with two Webster base runners on board.

The following day, the Texas Rangers choose Kaase, who plays his college ball at Division III Texas Lutheran, in the twenty-third round of the Major League draft. Kaase will take some time to make his decision and play a month in the NYCBL before signing with the big-league club. He will finish the summer playing rookie ball in the Arizona League and return to college in the fall.

Kaase joins several current and former NYCBL players taken in the 2007 MLB draft. It is a banner year as twenty-six NYCBLers hear their names called. Along with Kaase, Zach Lutz, Chris Garcia, Jose Made and Tom Edwards also go in the draft.

Lutz, taken in the fifth round by the New York Mets, signs and will play the summer for the Brooklyn

Cyclones of the New York-Penn League. The Angels take Garcia in the fifteenth. Made goes to the Cubs in the twentieth, and Edwards goes to the Rangers in forty-first.

Jordon Herr also gets selected. The summer before, Herr played in the Webster organization when the team was called the Rochester Royals. The son of former major leaguer Tommy Herr goes in the forty-first round to the Cubs.

The Brockport owner, Stan Lehman, gives the starting lineups over the public address system. Meanwhile, head coaches Kelly and Jim Maciejewski meet with umpires Leon Cyrus and James Salamone to discuss the ground rules and exchange lineups. After a couple moments of banter, the coaches return to their respective dugouts, and it is time to play ball.

Mark Stuckless leads off for Webster. The lanky outfielder from Kanata, Canada reaches first on an error. Shortstop, Gary Helmick follows. He hits the second pitch foul down the left-field line and splits his bat. Quickly, Helmick returns to the dugout and retrieves a new piece of lumber. He fouls the third pitch off the back stop. Again, he breaks his bat. He hesitates. The Towson University stars needs a new bat, but he has only brought two, and both have turned to splinters.

"Does someone have a 33? My others are in the car," whispers Helmick, not wanting to draw attention to his misfortune.

McIntyre helps him scour the bat rack before Helmick finds something suitable.

As he returns to the batter's box, one of teammates mumbles under his breath: "You don't suppose he can break three in one at bat?"

Helmick doesn't break another bat...at least not until the ninth game.

One out later, Santos doubles home Stuckless. Fellow North Carolina A & T teammate, McIntyre, doubles and Santos scores. Webster will not score again until the ninth when Rob Lawler leads off with a single and advances to second on a wild pitch. Lawler scores on Johnson's single.

Pullyblank takes the hill for Kelly's team. The right-hander from Caledonia, New York is a rugged-looking pitcher. Not tall, he fills out his frame with wide shoulders and a solid torso. It is as if he heard the word strapping used to describe Curt Schilling, his boyhood hero then playing for the Philadelphia Phillies, and ran to a dictionary. Upon reading "powerfully built, robust," he decided the description fit, and that was what he would be. Pullyblank rocks and pivots on the pitcher's mound with a corkscrew delivery.

"The Caledonia Kid" is today's tough-luck loser. He surrenders three runs. Two runs come on a home run by Will Rodriguez in the second inning. The frame starts with Eric Ferguson reaching base on an error. Rodriguez follows. The home run gets over the 340 foot sign in right-center field. Kelly, who played two years at Brockport State, quips: "That's the jet stream out there," referring to the nickname created by the short distance from home plate to the fence. By comparison, right center-field the following night at Sal Maglie Stadium is 375 feet from the batter's box.

From that point, Pullyblank pitches like someone has taken the jam from his donut. He strikes out the next two batters and retires a third sawing off his bat. He sets down the next twelve batters in a row. A seeing-eye single in the sixth breaks up the streak.

During the seventh-inning stretch, former Riverbat coach Jason Bunting is brought onto the field and presented a plaque honoring him as the 2006 NYCBL Coach-of-the-Year. One day later, Texas also takes the ace of Bunting's high school staff, Brian Dupra, in the 36th round of the Major League Baseball draft. Two days later, Bunting, Dupra and the Greece Athena Trojans suffer a heart-breaking loss in the state semi-finals to North Rockland High.

Whether motivated by habit or clinging to hope, Kelly sends Gardner and Brown to warm up in the pen during the eighth. Despite the ninety degree air, Gardner dons a heavy, hooded sweatshirt and begins his warm-up. It is all for naught. Webster fails to tie the score in the ninth.

Kelly gathers the team together before sending them on their own. He reinforces that he will treat the players as men. "We will not carry on about your mistakes. This is a long season. You are here to get a chance to improve. We will give you every opportunity to do that."

There is a visible spirit of enthusiasm in the eyes of these players as they look to their coach. They come from places like Bristol, Tennessee and Archbold, Ohio. Some travel from Fuquay Varina, North Carolina and even the tiny Caribbean island of Curacao. They have come to Upstate New York. They come chasing a dream. Each brings their own spirit. A spirit that can be traced through generations of young baseball players.

David Halberstam refers to this kindred spirit in his book, *Summer of '49.* Halberstam narrates the dramatic pennant chase of the Boston Red Sox, Cleveland Indians and the New York Yankees. In his opening chapter he writes: "When a poor American boy dreamed of escaping his grim life, his fantasy probably involved becoming a professional baseball player. It was not so much the national sport as binding national myth."

While many of the players in the NYCBL are not poor, they aspire to the "myth" of baseball. They come to Upstate New York leaving behind their college campuses, aluminum bats and, for many, their families to hone their wares in hopes of fulfilling a dream. This league serves as a conduit to this dream. While the names of Sullivan, Helmick, Carmody, Offerman and Curynski will only share space with DiMaggio and Williams on the pages of this book, these individuals share a spirit.

For the New York Yankees that spirit created the "Yankee Mystique:" veteran players expounding the virtues of hard work and preparation to attain success. For professional players of the 1940's, success on the field meant the possibility of a better life. It is hard to imagine, but the salaries of professional athletes of the post-World War II era were measured in thousands rather than millions. The great Joe DiMaggio created a stir amongst the Yankee front office when he requested a salary of $100,000. Eventually, the front office relented and paid the "Yankee Clipper" his due.

The average salary of the time ranged from $9,000 to $12,000. While more than acceptable for the standard of living during the time period, it did not give ball players the chance to rest and recover during the off-season. Rather, many big leaguers supplemented their income with winter jobs. That is unless one could play on a pennant-winning team. Finishing first in the American or National League meant a bonus check in the area of $5,000. For many, the sum meant the possibility of attaining such necessities as a house, a new car or college tuition for a child. The bonus check provided a comfortable lifestyle. A comfortable lifestyle offered the chance to recover from nagging injuries and the opportunity to prolong a career. The possibility of a World Series bonus created a spirit of urgency.

The players of the NYCBL share that spirit. For many of these 21st Century college players the league represents their first foray into the use of wood bats. They will experience increased competition measured by forty-two games in less than two months. They will get a taste of traveling between games on the roads of

Upstate New York. All this the players subscribe to for the chance to be seen by a big-league scout. The possibility of hearing their name called in the MLB draft creates their level of urgency.

Winning plays an important role for these Webster Yankees. Similarly, winning was important to the New York Yankees. Winning for Tommy Heinrich meant a new house. Winning for these Yankees means the possibility of making the post-season. The top four teams in both the NYCBL East and West divisions will make the playoffs. Qualifying for those playoffs means increased opportunities to be scouted.

It is Opening Day and, as the saying goes, "Hope springs eternal." These college athletes will settle into their new surroundings. They will adjust their swings to wood bats. They might even adjust their attitude about the "myth" of baseball before the season finishes.

Kelly finishes his post-game comments. Players depart the field and head for the parking lot. Some of the local players have friends and family in attendance. A few former coaches wait to chat with ex-players. Sullivan stops to talk to Ory Mee, his high school coach.

It's off to Niagara tomorrow, then on to Scio and Bolivar before an off-day on Monday. Possibilities await.

New York Collegiate Baseball League
Webster Yankees at Brockport Riverbats
Jun 7, 2007 at Brockport, NY (Clark Whited BB Comp)

Webster Yankees 3 (0-1)

Player	AB	R	H	RBI	BB	SO	PO	A	LOB
Stuckless lf	4	1	0	0	0	0	1	0	1
Helmick ss	4	0	0	0	0	0	4	3	0
Santos 1b	4	1	2	1	0	0	7	2	0
McIntyre rf	3	0	1	1	0	0	1	1	1
Lawler 2b	3	1	1	0	1	1	0	2	0
Johnson cf	3	0	1	1	1	0	3	0	2
Nidiffer dh	1	0	0	0	1	1	0	0	0
Stifler c	4	0	0	0	0	1	6	2	1
Sullivan 3b	4	0	0	0	0	1	1	1	1
Pullyblank p	0	0	0	0	0	0	1	0	0
Totals	30	3	5	3	3	4	24	11	6

Brockport Riverbats 6 (1-0)

Player	AB	R	H	RBI	BB	SO	PO	A	LOB
Sumner, Rob cf	2	1	0	0	1	1	1	0	0
Benham, Chris cf	1	0	0	0	0	0	0	0	0
Gardner, Andy dh	3	2	1	1	1	1	0	0	0
Kaase, Jake ss	4	1	3	2	0	0	2	7	0
Muoio, Steve 1b	3	0	1	1	1	0	17	1	0
Dudley, Aaron c	4	0	1	0	0	0	5	0	0
Moley, Randy rf	4	0	0	0	0	1	0	0	3
Ferguson, Eric lf	2	1	0	0	1	0	0	0	0
Rodriguez, Will 3b	3	1	1	2	0	1	0	3	0
Abrams, Jeff 2b	3	0	0	0	0	1	2	8	0
Maxwell, Rob p	0	0	0	0	0	0	0	1	0
Yager, Austin p	0	0	0	0	0	0	0	1	0
Brown, Matt p	0	0	0	0	0	0	0	0	0
Totals	29	6	7	6	4	5	27	21	3

```
Score by Innings                     R  H  E
-------------------------------------------
Webster Yankees..... 200 000 001 -  3  5  3
Brockport Riverbats. 220 000 02X - 6  7  3
-------------------------------------------
```

E - Santos; McIntyre 2; Benham; Kaase; Rodriguez. DP - Riverbats 4.
LOB - WY
6; Riverbats 3. 2B - Santos 2; McIntyre; Gardner; Kaase. HR - Rodriguez. HBP
- McIntyre; Nidiffer 2. CS - Kaase; Ferguson.

Webster Yankees	IP	H	R	ER	BB	SO	AB	BF
Pullyblank...................8.0		7	6	3	4	5	29	33

Brockport Riverbats	IP	H	R	ER	BB	SO	AB	BF
Maxwell, Rob...............3.1		3	2	1	2	2	13	16
Yager, Austin 4.2		0	0	0	1	0	12	15
Brown, Matt.................1.0		2	1	1	0	2	5	5

Win - Yager (1-0). Loss - Pullyblank (0-1). Save - BrownM (1).
WP - Pullyblank; BrownM. HBP - by Maxwell (Nidiffer); by Yager
(McIntyre); by
Yager (Nidiffer). PB - Stifler; Dudley.
Umpires - HP: Leon Cyrus 1B: James Salamone
Start: 5:00p Time: 2:30 Attendance: 102

Chapter 2
Winter Wouldn't Let Go This Year

The picture on the front page of the Webster Yankee website lacked promise: a snow-covered field with a few trees cut down, a foot bridge over a non-distinct creek, a gully and a front-end loader lurking ominously in the background. The caption read: "The ground is being laid for what will soon be the new home of the Webster Yankees NYCBL baseball team!" The picture, taken in the first week of April, added the cliché insult to injury for any western New Yorker who had endured another endless winter.

Baseball fans looking for banks of lights, bleachers, a scoreboard and any semblance of a diamond went away disappointed. Instead, patrons received another reminder of a winter which began in western New York when a record snowfall submerged Buffalo during the last week of October. Schools closed. Power companies came from across the state to assist the thousands of households left without service. Halloween offered only tricks for the children of the Queen City, a nickname given to Buffalo because it is the second largest city on the Great Lakes next to Chicago.

In February, five straight days of squalls dropped more than 100 inches of snow in Oswego County. The storm made national news. Pictures of residents entering and exiting their homes through second-story windows made an indelible impression on news watchers.

Situated between Oswego and Buffalo, on the northeast side of Rochester, Webster did not make the national news for record snow falls. Rather, it received the tail end of both storms and a few others. The record snowfalls of winter arrived after the third wettest September on record. Soggy conditions made work outside difficult and, at times, treacherous. Large construction vehicles sat dormant waiting for firm ground to support the weight of such massive machines.

The delay gave the Department of Environmental Conservation ample time to reconsider the plot of land designated as home field for the Webster Yankees. The parcel was deemed a necessary wetland area for many species of birds and other wild life. Lawyers were brought in. Discussions ensued and a decision to cease work resulted. The agreement seemed simple and logical. Natural habitat should not be disturbed. Webster was a large enough community that finding a new location seemed possible.

When news of the decision became public, Mark Perlo and Mike Kelly were already well entrenched in their preparations for the upcoming season. The cease-work order meant the Webster Yankees would play back-to-back games in the same location only three times over the course of the forty-two game schedule.

They did not have time to consider any potential consequences for not having a clubhouse that the team could
call its own during the summer. They lacked permanent
space to house the team's equipment. They would go
without a concession stand and refrigerator to keep hot
dogs and drinks between home games. The timing of
the decision created a ripple effect to be endured
throughout the season. Undaunted, the owner and general manager/coach forged ahead. Both relied heavily
on a network of contacts and friends as they prepared
for the 2007 campaign.

For Perlo, a successful businessman, the idea of
owning an amateur baseball team presented an opportunity to give back to his community and to a game he
loved. Perlo grew up in Webster. He attended Webster
schools before moving on to Monroe Community College. There he met Coach H. David Chamberlain, the
current NYCBL commissioner, and his life changed.
With a head covered in dangling locks and an unshaven
face, Perlo walked on to the baseball diamond at
Monroe in the fall of 1976. After that first practice,
Chamberlain suggested that Perlo make a trip to the
barber's shop. Like any teenager, Perlo originally bris-
tled at any such notion. Eventually his love for baseball
won out, and a clean-shaven, neatly-groomed Perlo returned the next day. He went on to play first base and
in 1978 served as the captain of the Monroe team that
qualified for the Junior College World Series.

Along the way, Chamberlain taught Perlo the life-long lessons of commitment, team work and dedication - lessons that Perlo uses to this day.

After two years at Monroe, Perlo moved on to Niagara University. He earned a degree in Business Administration. From there, he took a job with the Xerox Corporation and worked banging on doors for his next sale. Perlo covered the area south of Rochester from Henrietta to Dansville.

Two decades later, Perlo employs fifty. His company, Xerographic Solutions, Incorporated, sells office equipment to businesses from Erie, Pennsylvania to Syracuse, New York. The kid with an unshaven face and dangling locks now runs a company that earned revenues of $15,000,000 in its seventeenth year of existence.

Having lived a lifetime in and around Rochester, Perlo questioned how such a vibrant community failed to offer a major sports team. He watched as Buffalo, seventy miles to the west, supported major league teams in both the NHL and NFL. Syracuse, ninety miles to the east, enjoyed division one college sports.

Save for the forays of the Rochester Royals basketball team in the then National Basketball League and the Rochester Lancers in the North American Soccer League, Rochester's sports community feasted on the minor league accomplishments of the Rochester Red Wings, one of the original teams from the International

Baseball League (AAA), the Rochester Americans of the American Hockey League and other minor league teams such as the Rattlers and Knighthawk lacrosse teams and the Rochester Rhinos of A-League soccer . Rochester proved its love for sports when Baseball America nominated the Flower City as Baseball City USA.

The city lacked the major sports attraction it deserved. Before 2005, when the Rochester Institute of Technology entered NCAA Division I sports with their men's hockey team, the city's exposure to top collegiate talent was limited to occasional games at the War Memorial featuring the visiting St. Bonaventure Bonnies or the Syracuse Orange.

Perlo saw the NYCBL as a chance to bring top college athletes into the area. His team would consist not only of players from all over the country, but also opposing teams would visit with their wide array of talent. Perlo and Kelly agreed to build the nucleus of their roster around local talent, and add to the lineup with the best possible talent they could find outside of Rochester. Rochester-area players got a chance to improve and showcase their talents. Local fans had the opportunity to see some great baseball. The fit seemed perfect. With that the Rochester Royals came into being and began play in the 2006 NYCBL season.

For Perlo, Mike Kelly was an obvious choice as coach. Kelly, too, played at Monroe. Both learned how to play the game from Coach Chamberlain, and Perlo had confidence in the young, enthusiastic coach. Testament to Kelly's commitment was his demand to also serve as general manager of the team. He wanted to build his own roster of players. Kelly also knew the team did not have a field to call home and leaving a baseball diamond the way it was found or better is something Kelly understood. He also knew the possible consequences of being the head coach. If things were not where they were supposed to be, eventually the phone call of discontent would reach his desk. Kelly was well aware of the duties. He chose to accept those burdens.

With veteran minor leaguer, Dave Brust, as his assistant Kelly put together a club in 2006 that won nineteen of their last twenty-three games to qualify for the league playoffs. Once there, a walk-off home run in the third and decisive game in the first round of the playoffs ended the Royals' season.

Encouraged by the results of that first season, Perlo and Kelly eagerly looked forward to the 2007 season. The team's success captured the attention of Senator Mike Nozzolio. As a fan of baseball and a fan of the league, Nozzolio offered his support and help for the young franchise. Having the team move into his jurisdiction allowed the Senator to allocate money to the team. Nozzolio's district included Webster and the Yankees came into being.

Moving to Webster made sense. Beside the fact that Perlo grew up in the community of over 40,000 residents, Webster earned recognition as a sports town. In 2003, Sports Illustrated nominated Webster as SI's #1 Sports Town for New York State. The community's commitment to sports was evidenced by its high school football team. After winning class AA state titles in 1999 and 2001, the one school divided into two. Without so much as skipping a beat, Webster-Schroeder went on to win the 2002 state title. Since then the two schools, Webster-Schroeder and Webster-Thomas, have played against each other four times in sectional championship games. It was a town known for collaboration between community and school.

Owning the Webster Yankees gave Perlo an opportunity to put lessons learned into play as he ventured into the arena of owning a summer college baseball team. When asked of his role as team owner, Perlo jokes: "I am the chief fund-raiser." The successful businessman returned to banging on doors. Now, Perlo banged on doors seeking sponsors for his team.

Perlo needed funds to pay umpire fees, team travel expenses, uniforms, bats, balls and to maintain a web site. The team needed to provide league fees and field usage fees. The owner also had the obligation to find housing for eleven players coming from out-of-town. This was no easy task. Many of the more-established teams in the league, such as Hornell and Watertown, generated a list of potential host families.

Hosting a player is a two-month commitment. For a team like Webster starting from scratch, it is a challenge to find people willing to make such a sacrifice. Perlo called on Brian DiNardo. DiNardo's contribution showed the business ties Perlo had developed in the community.

The owner of Oakmonte Apartments, provided two luxury condominiums for up to eight players. The guys staying at the apartment complex in Webster had access to an indoor fitness room, an outdoor pool and various other amenities. Beyond that, Perlo would not have to worry about player complaints regarding the living conditions.

By the time he finished, Perlo had his sponsors: John Burt from Power Management, Gary Mauro from JT Mauro Plumbing, Arunas Chesonis from PAETEC Communications and Gary Polisseni from the Polisseni Agency combined for the $30,000 the Yankees required to make a go of it.

Meanwhile, Kelly was busy putting together his roster. He needed each player to sign a contract committing himself to the Webster Yankees for the 2007 season. To be eligible a player must have played at least one year of college baseball and have at least one year of college eligibility remaining. A summer team can only roster a maximum of five players from any particular college. Further, a player is not eligible to participate with a summer team if his college coach works for the team.

The sometimes delicate task of compiling a roster requires frequent communication because there is not a clearly defined pool of players eligible to play in the league. The players do not enter their name into a draft. Rather, college coaches and summer coaches involve themselves in an intricate process of player evaluations.

College coaches understand the NYCBL status. Summer collegiate leagues divide into three unofficial tiers. The first tier consists of the Cape Cod and Alaska leagues. These two leagues have produced the largest list of players who have gone on to enjoy professional careers. Mark Teixeira, Craig Biggio and Jason Varitek all spent at least one summer on The Cape. Craig Counsell, Frank Thomas and Randy Johnson each honed their wares in the midnight sun of the Alaska League. The New England Collegiate, Valley, Texas and Northwoods make up the second tier of summer college baseball leagues.

The NYCBL is a high-ranking third tier league; which translates, in part, to the big schools sending athletes in need of game-playing experience. Many of these kids play on college teams where they are not yet personally responsible for the wins and losses. Getting these kids to take pride in a victory and take a defeat to heart is part of the summer baseball experience. Kelly accepts the challenge of getting players to mature, but he depends on schools sending kids who want to play and learn the game of baseball.

The two parties seek a balance. Colleges want their kids getting appropriate playing time while summer teams want to compete and develop talent. This balance can be easily upset. If a field player does not play in a position of his liking or get enough at bats, he returns to school unhappy. He will talk, and others might not want to play for that summer team in the future. If a pitcher doesn't get his innings, the summer could be seen as a waste of time and not worthy of a future commitment. A player might not enjoy the overall experience of the summer: poor living accommodations, homesickness and personality conflicts all enter into the equation. Likewise, if a college coach sends a player more interested in a vacation than working on his game, the summer coach and general manager might hesitate in taking a player from that school in the future. At the same time, coaches do not want to burn bridges as future players or situations might work out better. Any coach worth his salt will take all these variables into consideration when organizing a roster.

Kelly understands the monster. He knows the kids on this team are not his kids. These players could easily be one and done; come to Webster, play one season, return to campus and move on to another summer team next year. A college coach, particularly at a four-year school, has the opportunity to establish a long-range plan with a kid. This involves a student-athlete getting an education and developing on the diamond over a period of years.

Summer coaches work in terms of months or maybe even just weeks. They need to make a good first impression and establish a rapport with the players quickly. At the same time, Kelly wants to develop baseball players and good citizens. It is a job he takes to heart. Among other things, he wants to see batters move the runner along, see his defense line up a cut-off and watch his infield execute the defense of a bunt.

Simultaneously, he needs to have enough players to compete in a NYCBL schedule that regularly consists of six games per week. He cannot go without an appropriate number of arms in his bullpen and starting rotation. Consideration must be given to adequate recovery time between outings, but he also must make sure each pitcher gets enough work and regular work.

He also has to consider field players. The roster needs enough guys to cover a smooth rotation for each position, keeping in mind all the time the possibility of injuries, family emergencies and the human element of dealing with young men trying to make up their minds about life. Still, Kelly understands how a consistent infield can serve as a foundation for the team. In this brief period the young coach needs to develop teamwork.

Players want to prove themselves as individuals and attract the attention of professional scouts. Kelly recognizes this and allows them the freedom to be aggressive even to the point of making mistakes. At the same time, Kelly stresses that scouts like to watch winning teams. The better the team performs the better the chance for each individual to succeed.

Over time, Kelly has created a network of fellow coaches that share a mutual understanding. Traveling as an assistant coach with Monroe Community College, he developed a rapport with Scott Roane at Towson University. Formerly the head coach at Dundalk Community College, Roane met Kelly when Monroe made its annual trip south to play its early spring season. Both Gary Helmick and Jason Stifler came from Towson, and the two made positive contributions in 2006. Kelly made the call early to Roane to secure both players. Helmick signed right away; Stifler hesitated. While certainly Helmick's infield position plays an important role in the success of a team, Kelly knew he would have some flexibility at shortstop, second and third base. The position of catcher lacks that flexibility. Not many kids can easily adjust to the role of a team's back stop. The indecision created a dilemma. The problem resolved itself when Stifler eventually decided to spend another summer with Webster. Roane also wanted to get Josh Brown some innings. The right-hander pitched in the Valley League the past summer but academic ineligibility kept him off the mound for the duration of the '06-'07 season.

Adam "Bomber" Curynski, Adam Perlo and Mark Stuckless all signed in October. Coming from Monroe, Kelly had no problem tracking down and getting signatures from the pitcher, catcher and outfielder. Signing Perlo for a team owned by his dad was a no-brainer. Originally, Pullyblank, another Monroe kid, signed with Geneva but reconsidered after taking into account the ninety-minute commute from Caledonia to Geneva.

Shawn Bailey had to wait to sign. After redshirting his freshman year, he was unsure of his status for the next college year. According to league and NCAA rules, a student-athlete cannot play for his own coach. Eventually, Bailey joined the Yankees after accepting a scholarship from Division II powerhouse Mesa State. In this situation, Kelly and Perlo might have easily circumvented the rules and signed Bailey. Many expected them to take advantage of their relationship with Commissioner Chamberlain. But these men learned the game differently and Chamberlain accepted nothing less from his former players.

After signing the Monroe kids, Kelly quickly redirected his attentions. Offerman was a great kid and a great presence in the dugout for the Royals. Kelly e-mailed Gino directly to get a commitment. Gardner was another kid who played with the organization in '06. The southpaw showed limitless potential. He lived in the Rochester area and attended Ithaca. He sent word through his college coach, George Valesente. He wanted to play in 2007.

Next, Kelly focused on two more local kids: Veenema and Sullivan. Both attended the University of Rochester and played for Joe Reina, another former MCC guy and member of the Chamberlain coaching tree. Veenema and Sullivan played with the Riverbats the previous season when the organization was known as Genesee Valley. Sullivan played at Monroe his freshman year, and Veenema knew Kelly through inter-squad scrimmages. Both signed early. Veenema wanted to avoid the daily cross-county commute from Penfield to Brockport. Later, Veenema waffled when an opportunity came from the New England Collegiate League. Kelly had the pitcher's signed contract but offered a release if that was what Blair and his family wanted. Veenema decided to stay with Webster. Sullivan signed as a much-needed utility player.

In the mean time, Kelly exchanged e-mails with coaches at the University of Miami, Ohio, Austin Peay and Ball State. All had players weighing their options. Four Red Hawks from Miami played with the Royals in '06. Kelly hoped for a return engagement. None materialized. Players from the other schools also did not commit.

Cory Mee e-mailed. The University of Toledo head coach had ties to the Rochester area. He grew up and played in the suburb of Hilton before going on to star at the University of Notre Dame. Mee had two freshmen that needed work: Johnson and Bernath. Kelly sent the contracts through the mail.

Pat Carey from Iona College sent word. He had two, veteran starters. Webster had spots for both. Carmody and DiNuzzo signed.

Lawler signed through Mark Perlo.

Chris Chernisky, the head coach at Niagara University, contacted Kelly. He wanted to place Chris Coleman on the roster. Kelly added the lefty to his bullpen.

All the while, Kelly stayed in contact with Santos. Nelson played two years at Monroe before moving on to North Carolina A & T. Last season, Nelson played in the NYCBL with Geneva. He knew the Red-Wings coach Dave Herbst personally and gave it a try. Like Pullyblank, the commute deterred Santos. Nelson provided the best example of a five-tool player on the roster. He hit for average, hit for power, possessed good speed, a good glove and a strong arm. Santos also lured in his A & T teammate, McIntyre. By the end of the season the A & T duo played every inning of every game.

The team was taking shape as Kelly headed to the winter general managers' meeting. The coach was a little frustrated with not getting anyone from Miami and Ball State, but he had other options. He could afford to wait for kids who wanted to play.

In February, league president, Brian Spagnola, circulated an e-mail with a list of prospective players. The list piqued Kelly's interest because Nidiffer's name was on it… or maybe that Nidiffer was an available catcher grabbed the coach's interest. Only four months remained until opening day and Stifler had not yet signed. The Webster roster technically only had one backstop: Adam Perlo. Sullivan could play the position, but he had expressed an interest in being a utility player. An immediate concern is warming up guys in the bullpen. If Perlo is calling the game, and Sullivan playing the field, who would go to the pen with the relievers? Kelly needed another catcher and expressed interest. Much to the coach's surprise, Nidiffer did not immediately commit. Kelly had one catcher signed and offers out for two more. The skipper would bide his time.

Finally, Stifler and Nidiffer signed. Kelly went from not having enough catchers to having too many.

As the season drew near, Kelly made final preparations. He filled out the team order for bats through the D-Bat Company of Dallas, Texas. Which bats he gets are not as important as which bats he initially distributes. Making the adjustment from aluminum bats used during the college season to wood bats in the summer season is a challenge for young players.

Young players need to trust their hands and shorten their swings. While they learn the adjustment, Kelly doles out the ash bats. At nearly half the price as the maples, the softer ash allows the hitters a learning curve by limiting the number of broken bats. The tradeoff is that the ash bats have less pop than the maples.

Kelly's first order of six dozen bats will hold the team over until the all-star break. He gets an equal number of Pro-Stock and Pro-Cut ash, along with Stock and Pro Maple. The ash bats come in three different models: K9, J33 and 73D. The skipper carefully makes sure to order a wide variety of handles and knobs. Having an array of choices gives the players a chance to adjust and experiment as the season progresses. It also means some haggling over the bats. Players quickly try and lay claim. From time to time the coach will need to mediate.

D-Bat sends a pair of fungoes. Lighter, skinnier and longer, the fungoes are what Brust, Kelly and all coaches use to hit infield practice. The size of fungoes allows for more control helping a coach consistently get the desired effect: either a ground ball or pop fly. The light weight stick helps a coach's endurance considering most often it is one coach hitting to several fielders.

Kelly will wait on the maples. The kids get their chances with the harder bats in the third week of the season.

At the first practice, many of the bats come out of the box already flaking. Brust teaches the youngsters how to "bone" a bat. The term "boning" comes from players of past decades using a large, smooth bone, such as a femur, taken from a butcher to compress the wood of a bat. Nowadays a thick, glass bottle such as those used for soda or a heavy duty post will work. The process involves holding a bat with a hand on either end of the stick and drawing the lumber across a metal post such as at the end of a fence or backstop. Using the correct force will tighten the grains of the bat and help the lumber to last. "Boning" is mostly needed for ash bats. Maples come out of the box ready to use.

By the end of practice, Kelly realizes his need for another infielder. Bailey is still ineligible to play. The coach does not want to rush a kid, especially with such an important decision as a college choice. After practice, Kelly makes some inquiries. Help is on the way. Danny Bertolini is playing as a reserve in the Southern League. He is granted a release and arrives in time for the third game. Brad Hull, another outfielder, arrives at the same time. Hull's stay lasts less than five days. He aggravates a knee injury and returns home to Nebraska having played only two games.

Having the first four games of the season on the road served as a reprieve of sorts for Perlo and Kelly. Instead of worrying about the responsibilities of hosting games, the two used it as an opportunity to get their feet underneath them. Kelly's Honda Element becomes the official equipment locker for the team. The back hatch opens to a stack of white, rectangular boxes on the left holding the hack sticks. Royal blue boxes containing a dozen game balls, each made especially for the NYCBL by Diamond One, rest on the floor of the sport-utility vehicle. The canvas bag containing the batting practice pearls are tossed to the side. Another bag holds the batting helmets.

For the home opener at Webster-Thomas High School, the Yankees need to provide the chalker. Kelly shoe horns it into the Element. Somehow, he manages to squeeze in four thirty- gallon containers, two containers for each dugout. One holds ice and bags; the other cooler contains water.

Perlo arrives early. With his band of volunteers, he assembles a makeshift concession stand: four folding tables in a U-shape. Perlo lugs the Rubbermaid containers full of snacks and Webster Yankee souvenirs from the back of his family van. Somehow, the owner managed to get an old grill into his vehicle. Hot dogs will be cooking soon.

Opening night proves to be an exercise in patience. First, with no district employees on site, turning on the scoreboard presents a challenge. Perlo rented a portable public address system for the evening. It does not work. Earlier in the week, the workers renovated the dugouts, laying a new foundation of concrete. The bench areas are off-limits for the game.

Curynski makes it all worthwhile. The six foot, two hundred and fifteen pound right-hander gets the win against the Elmira Pioneers. Less than two months later, the Pios will sweep the Glens Falls Eagles and win the league championship. Tonight "Bomber" is Elmira's daddy. He tosses a complete game, striking out eight, walking three and allowing two runs. The pop he makes in the catcher's mitt might suggest his nickname. The moniker, though, came from Adam's surname which rhymes with the infamous Ted Kaczynski of "Unabomber" lore.

Johnson goes deep in the fourth. McIntyre raps two hits and drives in two runs. Webster wins 7-2.

After the game, with a bag of ice wrapped around his elbow, "Bomber" deflects all praise. He takes the time to note the team defense.

A few little leaguers linger getting their last autographs for the night.

Perlo and Kelly finish loading their vehicles. It was not exactly what they had in mind, but the team has two wins and three losses. The first day of summer is still more than a week away. The season shows promise.

Chapter 3

Slow Out Of The Gate

		R	H	E
Brockport	220 202 104	13	16	2
Webster	200 100 000	3	7	2

As bad as the line score appeared, it did not tell half of the story. The Yanks managed five hits in the last five innings, all singles. Johnson was the only runner to get beyond first. A week earlier the team faced a 14-0 deficit against Niagara but managed to score five runs before the end of the game. Today, they flat-lined.

Webster had every reason to be motivated for this game. More than any other match-up on their ledger this had the character of a civil war. Most teams in the league listed fewer than six players from New York State on their roster. The combined rosters of Webster and Brockport consisted of twenty-four players from the Empire State. Of these, seventeen lived within the Monroe County boundary. Ten of those players were current or former teammates at MCC. Joe Davis, the Brockport starter, played two years at MCC before moving on to the University of Hawaii-Hilo. Two more Riverbats, Steve Muoio and Dom Sapp, helped MCC to the Junior College World Series scarcely a month prior to the match-up with Brockport. Now, they sat in their dugout and looked across the field at an opponent that boasted five players from that MCC band of brothers.

Rivalries continued from there. Gardner played at Ithaca with Brockport's Eric Ferguson. If that was not enough, Gardner's younger brother, Andy, was the starting catcher for the "Bats."

On the surface, it appeared as a game between two teams divided by a thirty-mile stretch along Route 104. Beneath the surface a blood feud simmered.

Brockport held bragging rights because of the Opening Day triumph. Instead of using the familiarity as incentive to feed their competitive appetite, Webster seemed intent on ignoring the challenge facing them for the day.

An hour before the first pitch the day's starter, DiNuzzo, lounged in the locker room. He had yet to put on his game uniform and looking at him one would have guessed pre-game warm-up was something of a passing fancy at best. At one point, Kelly looked at his starter and commented: "Bobby? You do know you're starting today?" DiNuzzo chuckled and continued his part in a story of last night's escapades.

In his previous outing, against the first-place Allegany County Nitros, Bobby D. threw eight innings giving up two runs on five hits. The Stony Point native walked none, had five strike outs, a wild pitch, and he hit one batter. Unfortunately, Doug Ciallela, the Nitro starter, was a little better.

Ciallela earned NYCBL Player-Of-The-Day honors in his first start of the season. Ironically, when Nitro head coach, Brandon Scott, was asked for his lineup to be used in the online play-by-play broadcast, he made a

point to pronounce the last names of all his bullpen. He
was sure his young starter wouldn't last the duration.
Instead, his right-hander from Fairfield University
tossed a complete game shutout.

Kelly hoped *his* young right-hander might have a
repeat of his performance against the first-place Nitros.
He was sure the sticks could come through today.

Soon after DiNuzzo's first pitch, hopes were
dashed. Brockport's leadoff hitter, Chris Benham,
doubled into the gap in left-center. He later moved to
third on a wild pitch. One out later, Eric Ferguson
knocked his first of three doubles and six hits on the
day. Ferguson drove in his first of seven runs for the
day, a feat that broke the league's record of six. He
earned NYCBL Player-Of-The-Day Honors.

Another batter and DiNuzzo issued his second
wild pitch. Aaron Dudley worked a walk. With runners
on the corners, Chad King drilled an RBI single. Dudley
moved up to second. Brockport 2 Webster 0.

Randy Moley dropped a perfectly executed sacrifice bunt, and the runners advanced to second and third.
The out was welcomed by Kelly and the Webster bench.
While Moley's bunt was smart baseball, it was a life pre-
server for a drowning pitcher. DiNuzzo struck out Rodriguez and somehow two runs seemed acceptable
when one considered how many Brockport could have
plated.

Unlike DiNuzzo's previous outing, Webster
wasted little time recovering the runs. Santos reached
on an error, and McIntyre lashed at a 2-0 pitch and put

it over the fence in right field. Brockport 2 Webster 2. The runs scored resembled resiliency, but any positives to be taken from McIntyre's hit proved fleeting.

In the top of the second, Riverbat center-fielder, Sean O'Bannion, slashed a shot over DiNuzzo's head. The ball momentarily hung in the air, and Johnson charged with reckless abandon. Heavy with top-spin the ball dropped sharply, fell for a single, and bounded past the outstretched glove of the diving Yankee center-fielder. By the time Sullivan, playing right field for the first time on the season, recovered the ball, O'Bannion stood at third.

On the surface, Johnson's play seemed worthy of merit. He hustled and made a spectacular dive. He dirtied his uniform in the process. Johnson's attempt might bring cheers for effort on a Sunday afternoon shagging flies with family or friends. The dive might even have been understandable given a different game situation. If the score was tied in the bottom of the ninth with a runner on third and two outs, the situation would make the dive a necessity. But in the second inning of a tie game, with one out and bases empty, the lunge was excessive. It was exactly the kind of play that continued to hinder the growth of this young team. Instead of limiting the possible damages, Johnson's decision made the situation worse.

DiNuzzo fanned the next batter. For a moment, the threat appeared to be averted. Could DiNuzzo take care of the situation? Could Bobby D. return to the form he had when he held Allegany County to two runs over eight innings? Jeff Abrams answered any remaining questions when he followed with a two-out walk. Ferguson strode to the plate and delivered both runners home with his second double in as many innings. Brockport 4 Webster 2.

The casual observer could suggest that Johnson's error made no difference. The runs scored in the inning would not differ based upon the center-fielder's poor judgment. But coming to the plate with one out and a runner on third is much different than one out and a runner on first. With a runner on third a deep fly ball scores a run whether the ball is caught or not. The batter can approach the situation a little more at ease, and a long fly out can become an extra-base hit if it gets in the gap. On the other hand, one out with a runner at first could be an inning-ending double play.

Johnson's play gave the momentum back to Brockport and caused a nagging doubt for Kelly. The play was an automatic for the coach. The outfielder needed to keep the ball in front of him and allow the team to make the necessary plays. Instead, the Yanks were back on their heels having to react rather than dictate the flow of the game.

DiNuzzo faced the minimum in the third, but the Webster bats made no noise. Andy Gardner led off the fourth with what amounted to a pop fly into right center field. Both Sullivan and Johnson converged on the ball. They made eye contact. They glanced at the ball and watched it drop. Not a word was spoken between the outfielders. Two innings prior Johnson dove for a ball that he needed to catch on one hop. Now, the young center-fielder let a fly ball drop for a leadoff single. O'Bannion sacrificed Gardner to second, and Benham followed with his third hit in four innings. After an Abrams bunt, Ferguson singled, and Benham scored Brockport's sixth run on the day.

DiNuzzo retired the side in order in the fifth, but the inning was his last. Kelly went to his bullpen and called on Bernath. Six to three in the fifth was not an insurmountable deficit, and Bernath pitched well in his last two appearances. The lanky left-hander allowed one unearned run in three and a third innings pitched against Niagara - a game in which the Power scored sixteen runs in the other five and two-thirds innings. The night prior, Bernath worked a perfect ninth inning against the Nitros. Maybe, just maybe, Bernath could stop the bleeding and give the Yankee bats a chance to recover.

With his second pitch Bernath hit Andy Gardner. Then, O'Bannion dropped a sacrifice bunt. Benham singled. Abrams struck out, and before Bernath induced a ground ball from Dudley, Ferguson drove in two more runs with a single.

In the seventh, Moley hit a one-out single. He moved to second on a wild pitch and scored when Gardner's two-out bunt bounded into no man's land past the pitcher and in front of the first baseman. McIntyre tried to scoop the ball with his glove and in one motion toss the ball to Bernath covering first. Instead, the toss landed in foul territory, and Moley scored on the play.

At first, the play looked like nothing more than another error. But it displayed the struggles facing Webster. If Moley hadn't advanced to second on the wild pitch, McIntyre would have been holding the runner on first, making it easier to field the ground ball and end the inning. Instead, he was playing back on the infield. McIntyre's indecision on the play represented Webster's situation. Now, even good players seemed to lack confidence. Like Johnson's error in the second McIntyre's ill-advised shuttle pass cost the Yankees another run. The next batter, O'Bannion, popped out to Bertolini, and the inning ended: Brockport 7 Webster 3.

Bernath, who gave up one unearned run in two outings last weekend, was charged with three runs in two innings of work. Kelly went to his bullpen again. This time he called on Gardner. The left-hander had become the team's stopper and a source of reliability. Earlier in the season, Gardner struck out seven consecutive batters and nine of eleven faced. At Dunn Field in Elmira, he spit nine seeds in the ninth and struck out the side. Gardner retired the side in the eighth, but he walked two, and it took an unorthodox double play to end the inning. With bases loaded, King hit a ground ball to third. Bailey picked it up, stepped on the bag and fired home to end the threat. For a moment there were signs of enthusiasm. Perhaps the inning-ending double play created a momentum shift.

Webster managed a two-out walk and a single in the bottom of the frame before the inning ended.

The misery continued in the ninth. Gardner returned to the mound and gave up a leadoff single to Moley. The next batter, Rodriguez, was zero for four with three whiffs. Gardner walked him. With runners on first and second, Gardner's younger brother, Andy, stepped in and promptly worked a walk to load the bases. O'Bannion followed with a single, and Moley scored the first earned run of the year off Gardner. On the play, Johnson missed the cut-off and another run scores. Brockport scored three runs before the inning ended.

In the bottom of the ninth, Sullivan fanned. Bertolini singled, and Bailey grounded into a game-ending double play: 4-6-3.

The loss dropped Webster to four and ten.

Prior to the game, Kelly waxed nostalgic with team owner, Mark Perlo: "Hey, we started six and eighteen and managed to make the playoffs last year. We can do it again this year. I'm not saying that I'm setting out to relive last year, but it does let us know what is possible."

After the game, Kelly wore a look of concern.

Three days ago, they beat Bolivar in extra innings to improve to three wins and seven losses. Kelly encouraged his team to break up the schedule into four-ten game seasons.

"We just finished our first ten games. I'm sure none of us planned to be three and seven, but that's where we are. Let's try and turn this around and go seven and three in our next ten games."

Urgency replaced encouragement.

Whether the players sensed their coach's anger, or they felt the sting of defeat, or they just wanted to get on with their post-game activities, the air in the locker room was decidedly different. Everyone sat quietly and motionless as Kelly spoke.

"I can't believe the programs some of you guys come from, and the plays that you make."

Kelly's words tore into the young athletes.

"We make pitches in counts that we have no business throwing. We don't make plays. I can guarantee you there is one thing I hate, and that is losing. I didn't bring you guys in here to lose. I am looking at a bunch of guys who have the talent to be drafted, but if you keep playing like this, no one is going to come and see you," said Kelly referring to big league scouts. "We are going to treat you like men. We are not going to nag you about mistakes. I have five available roster spots remaining. If I have to, I will bring in new players. That means less playing time for you guys. I don't want to do that, but I don't want to lose either."

For Brust, things had come to a head. Usually reserved, he allowed Kelly to address the group in situations like this. But he had too much to say. As a power-hitting third baseman and catcher he played three years of summer ball. He helped the Cohocton Red Wings to the league title in 1986. After that, he played two years in the Great Lakes Summer League. While there he earned a spot on the league's all-star team. Later, Brust played three years in the Atlanta Braves' system as a member of the Durham Bulls. The assistant coach had an idea as to the passion required to get to the next level. His words took on a Knute Rockne tone as he addressed the group.

"Other coaches comment how relaxed we are as a team. We are so relaxed I wanna vomit! We don't play baseball. We don't talk in the field; we don't hit our cutoffs; we can't move the runner; for cris'sake we can't bunt. WE CAN'T BUNT! We need to play each game as if it's our last. You need to treat each at bat, each play in the field as if it is your last. The fact is many of you are playing or will soon be playing your last games. You need to treat it that way and play with passion."

Brust's words hung over the silence of the room. A couple of nervous throats cleared. The only sound came from Brust as he grabbed his gym bag off the floor, shouldered the strap, walked from the room and down the left field line.

Kelly remained in the middle of the floor. His eyes cast down as he allowed the words of the veteran coach to sink in with the players. After what seemed like hours Kelly reminded the players of the next day's game in Niagara. They were to meet at the MCC parking lot and leave by 3p.m. for the hour drive.

As Kelly finished, the players quickly exited. Johnson was the first out of the locker room. The freshman usually changed into a comfortable pair of mesh shorts after a game. Today was different. Timely

46

flight was important. Others quickly followed. Bailey lingered and made a point to apologize to his coach for his late arrival at batting practice. Even owner Mark Perlo, who usually enjoyed staying and discussing the game, sensed the uncomfortable tone. He and friend Art Carlisi stood and listened outside the locker room. Both were veterans of many battles on athletic fields. The two decided that the team and coach needed space, and they headed to the parking lot.

Fifteen minutes later, Dugan Yard was empty save for Mike Kelly who lingered on with the perfunctory post-game clean up. With a push broom in hand he stood facing the first base dugout dragging the clay-colored dirt from the structure back onto the field. On this day, one could easily understand why Kelly might rush through this task. Instead, he patiently tended to the task at hand. He kicked up little, if any, dust as he worked his way from one end of the dugout to the other. Occasionally, he stopped, ran his fingers through his hair and stood one arm folded, hand holding the back of his neck – a man and his thoughts.

This is not what he planned when he cobbled together this roster. Helmick, Gardner, Stifler and Offerman all played key roles with the last year's push to the playoffs. Veenema and Sullivan gained valuable playoff experience with the Riverbats a season previous. Santos played with Geneva. All these guys had been through the battles before this summer. Kelly added a bunch of MCC kids: Bailey, Curynski, Pullyblank, Adam

Perlo and Stuckless. He expected more out of them. He didn't expect to be four and ten.

Three times today, his players failed to execute a sacrifice bunt - three times! In the third down four to two, Bailey led with a single. Stuckless was next - Stuckless, who played at Monroe. A player he had worked with for the last two seasons had a chance to move the runner into scoring position with one out. Instead, "Stucky" popped his bunt attempt in the air. It was caught, and Bailey doubled off first. Threat eliminated.

Sullivan led off the seventh with a single. After two failed attempts to move the runner, Bertolini had to swing away. He did and flied out to left. In the ninth, Sullivan struck out to the lead the inning. This time, Bertolini singled. Now, Bailey struggled at the plate. He too had to swing away and grounded into the game-ending double play. The inability to manufacture a run bothered the young coach.

A coach can easily find himself considering what if. What if we executed here? What if we made the play here? What if?

Today, those scenarios gnaw at Kelly.

Brockport, on the other hand, executed the sacrifice bunt on three occasions. Two of those runs crossed the dish. Add in two Webster errors, a missed cut off, three wild pitches, two hit batsmen, and it was not difficult to understand the ten-run deficit. Worse still was the fact that his players seemed to not care. With Veenema absent there was little chatter on the bench. Few were the shouts of encouragement for teammates.

Beyond that, Webster seemed completely out of synch. The heart of the order: Santos, McIntyre and Johnson managed one hit and one walk. The bottom of the order accounted for four hits, but none happened in the same inning. Sullivan singled in the fourth and seventh; Bertolini picked up a hit in the ninth and Bailey singled in the third. Only Sullivan generated a run when his base rap scored Lawler.

Johnson and Santos were of particular concern. Both had homered earlier in the season. Santos had extra base hits in each of the first three games. Since then, they both struggled. In only one game had the two managed to have multiple hits. Webster lost that game 17-11 to Niagara. Against Geneva, Bolivar and Elmira, all losses, these two in the Yankee lineup accounted for one hit.

After the previous weekend, this loss hurt. Last Saturday the pitching staff issued zero walks and the defense committed zero errors, but the offense scored zero runs. On Sunday, the offense scored eleven runs but the pitching staff walked seven, hit seven, and the defense committed four errors. At least last weekend parts were in place. There was reason to have hope. It seemed that time and patience would prevail. Today, Webster did their finest Patsy Cline and "fell to pieces."

The loss made the four wins seem like mirages. On June tenth, Webster beat Allegany County 9-1. The Nitros went on to win twenty of their next twenty-one. Two of those came at the expense of the Yankees. It was almost as if the win didn't happen. To make matters worse, through three head-to-head games Webster out-scored Allegany 11-7, yet the Nitros took two of three from the Yanks.

On June fourteenth, Webster handled Hornell 5-2. The schedule maker did not shine on the Dodgers. The night before Hornell was swept in a double-header at Geneva by the Red Wings. The first game went ten innings. The nightcap lasted eleven innings. By the time Hornell loaded the bus and traveled south on route 390 it was 2a.m. The next day was the annual school day at Maple City Park. The Hornell school district re-leased their elementary and middle school students for a special 11a.m. Hornell Dodgers' game. With less than nine hours between their arrival from Geneva and the first pitch against Webster, Hornell understandably lacked a competitive edge.

Six days and three losses later, Lawler ripped a two-out, walk-off double in the thirteenth as Webster beat one and eight Bolivar 4-3. A win is a win, but of all games this was one that Webster should have won run-ning away. Instead, the Yanks needed extra innings. A scheduling miscommunication caused Bolivar to arrive at the field less than thirty minutes before the sche-duled first pitch. Without any lights at Dugan Yard the first pitch could only be delayed until 5:30pm. Bolivar took the field without any pre-game batting practice. They were like lambs to the slaughter, except that Web-ster misplaced its knife. The game played out as a battle of attrition with the road-weary A's submitting in the thirteenth.

The one game that appeared real was the home opener. Adam "Bomber" Curynski tossed nine innings and limited the league's top-hitting team, the Elmira Pioneers, to seven hits and two runs. Helmick scored a pair, Johnson went yard, and McIntyre drove in a couple as the Yanks win 7-2. Other than a first inning hiccup, "Bomber" was in control all game. With a motion that appeared a jumble of flailing arms and legs, Curynski sawed bat handles and struck out eight.

Curynski gave Kelly someone with which he could rely. At six foot and two hundred and fifteen pounds "Bomber" is an imposing figure on the mound. "He is like something out of the 1940's," quipped Brust. "It is like he was working in a steel mill, and one day a scout walked in and asked for the biggest kid they had."

But "Bomber's" gem seemed like only a distant memory as Kelly turned the key and started up his Honda Element. He left Dugan Yard behind, but not the sting of defeat.

The next day, Webster travelled seventy-five miles west to their personal house of horrors, Sal Maglie Stadium. One day after the implosion, Pullyblank was scheduled to start against Niagara. The "Caledonia Kid" gave hope. He had two strong outings but came away with a loss and a no-decision. Pullyblank looked impressive in the opener against Brockport and left with the lead against Hornell in his second outing. Looking for someone else to lean on, Kelly wanted seven innings out of his starter. What he got was something drastically different.

While going through his pre-game bullpen session, Pullyblank knew something was wrong. He threw three pitches, none of which made it to his bullpen mate, Stifler. He stopped his preparations and told Kelly he couldn't pitch.

Kelly had two concerns. His first was for the welfare of his young starter. Pullyblank pitched for MCC the previous season. Kelly had come to know the young gun and respected his competitive fire.

The skipper's second concern rested with finding a spot starter, and the alternative did not look promising. Kelly wanted to get his young staff on a schedule, and the only arm ready was the dependable Gino Offerman. Gino was a great kid. He would do anything the team needed without complaining, including accepting a spot start less than fifty minutes before the first pitch. Gino pitching at Sal Maglie Field did bode well for the pinstripes. Gino was a ground-ball pitcher. The playing surface at Sal Maglie Stadium resembled a cow pasture. With its clumps of infield grass and ground hardened by a lack of watering, it played more like the "Plinko" board on "The Price Is Right" than an infield. Ground balls could not get a true bounce. Like the game show what would seem like a routine play turned into the ball bouncing every which way like a "Plinko" disc. Kelly had no other choice. Gino started.

At first, luck shone on the Webster nine. Santos and McIntyre both reached base with "Plinko" hits. Webster scored two in the first and one in the second for a three to one lead. Perhaps, Webster would get some breaks.

Any luck proved ephemeral. Offerman gave up six hits and eight runs in two and two-thirds. He walked one and hit three. For the second time, Niagara struck in the third inning against Webster. On June eighth, the Power scored eight unearned against Veenema in the third. They scored seven against Offerman and Coleman in the third stanza. Niagara 16 Webster 7.

For Pullyblank, the concern was as tangible as his throbbing arm. In his most recent start, he felt an unsettling difference in his arm. Initially he ascribed the "dead arm" feeling to his summer job. Spending the summer months making money painting houses, required the young right-hander manually to sand parts of some houses before painting. Perhaps the frequent repetitive motion wore out his arm.

But he knew better than that.

The right-hander traced the injury back to his freshman year at LeMoyne College. Coming out of tiny Caledonia-Mumford High School, Pullyblank eagerly looked ahead to a career at the central New York school. Nestled just outside of Syracuse, the Jesuit school regularly contended for the Metro Atlantic Athletic Conference title and a trip to the College World Series. Despite a student body of less than 4,000, the baseball program boasted an impressive list of players selected in the Major League draft.

Pullyblank wanted to be a part of this. During his freshman year, he earned a spot in the starting rotation. His starts came during mid-week games – more than acceptable for a freshman. He seemed on track for success until many of his starts were rained out. Instead of getting his chance to impress, Pullyblank spent a rainy spring watching from the bullpen. Like any young man he wanted to prove his abilities. This included over-throwing during his few opportunities.

He ignored any discomfort and focused on the short-term goal of becoming a weekend starter for Le-Moyne.

"The Caledonia Kid" pitched the 2006 summer for the Manchester Silk Worms of the New England Collegiate Baseball League. After working as reliever early in the season, Pullyblank earned a role as a starter. The experience rejuvenated his confidence. Then news reached him that LeMoyne's number one and two starters would return for another season. Pullyblank reconsidered his college choice. He didn't want to take the chance on spending another season on the sideline. He wanted to play the game he loved. Pullyblank called Skip Bailey at MCC and got a position on the Tribune staff. It was a detour by choice.

Now, Pullyblank took another detour but not by choice. When the soreness persisted, he scheduled an MRI. The diagnosis was exactly what he feared: a torn ulnar collateral ligament, a pitcher's nightmare. The injury required surgery and six to twelve months of rehab.

The diagnosis could not have come at a more inopportune time. The University of Louisiana-Monroe offered the right-hander a scholarship to finish his college career pitching in the Sun Belt Conference. Pullyblank visited the campus in northern Louisiana. Before signing, he needed to make sure all of his college credits transferred. In the mean time, the injury occurred. The young man knew he would need to be honest with his future coach, Jeff Schexnaider. Schexnaider reciprocated: the scholarship would still be available if Pullyblank proved his ability after the lengthy rehabilitation process. Until then, Pullyblank's career endured another detour.

Monday was an off day. Webster had plenty of wounds to lick. They were in seventh place - five games out of the playoffs, with a record of four wins and eleven losses.

Chapter 4

A Brief History of the NYCBL

In Phil Alden's *Field of Dreams,* a road-weary Ray Kinsella (played by Kevin Costner) and Terence Mann (played by James Earl Jones) happen upon a hitch-hiker. Looking for any "karma" they can get, Kinsella and his travelling mate invite the youth into their Volkswagen van. After a brief exchange of greetings, the bright-eyed Archie Graham announces: "I play baseball! I'm lookin' for a place to play. I heard that all through the Midwest they have towns with teams. And in some places they'll even find you a day job, so you can play nights and weekends." The youngster's description from the movie fits the essence of the NYCBL.

As described by league publicist, John McGraw, on the front page of its website, the New York Collegiate Baseball League, founded in 1978, is a summer wood bat development league for professional baseball. Major League Baseball funds a small portion of the league's annual budget. The league gives college players who have not yet signed a professional contract the opportunity to develop their skills at a higher level of play, gain experience with wood bats and be evaluated by scouts. The NYCBL is located in scenic upstate New York.

Enjoying a game in the NYCBL is like picking a restaurant. One can opt for any number of chain restaurants. These eateries are conveniently located on main thoroughfares or near any number of malls. A neon sign beckons patrons from miles away. Menus and service at such establishments follow the requirements dictated by a regional corporate office. Employees at these companies punch a clock to receive their hourly wages.

On the other hand, you can choose a family-owned establishment. These restaurants represent part of the local fabric. Often times, these places are a little out of the way. Word-of-mouth and reputation are their best advertisement. You go there once or twice, and the employees learn your name. You are not just a customer but part of the family. The Bayside and Proietti's in Webster are two restaurants that fit this bill. After just one visit, a customer will always return for more.

NYCBL fields are off the beaten path. First time fans might need directions to find the various fields. Sometimes, seeing the lights from a distance can capture the curiosity of a baseball fan. Once there, fans can enjoy an intimate experience - an experience that many may have thought not possible in the 21st century. Coaches and players are approachable. Owners often partake in the fund-raising. It is an inviting atmosphere for every fan.

Rudy Tucci served as the original commissioner of the NYCBL, and the Syracuse Chiefs (no affiliation with the Triple-A team) won the first two league titles. Since then teams have come and gone, but the league remains. The Broome Rangers amassed seven league titles from 1980 to 1991. The Cortland Apples took the title in '82. Ithaca's Lakers won three titles as did the Cohocton Red Wings. Brust led the Red Wings '86 title team. The Geneva Knights, Newark Raptors and Rome Indians all won one championship and then moved on from the league.

The NYCBL is part of the National Alliance of College Summer Baseball (NACSB) which oversees the competition of seven other leagues: the Central Illinois Collegiate League (CICL), Great Lakes Summer Collegiate League, Atlantic Collegiate Baseball League(ACBL), the Florida Collegiate Summer League (FCSL), Southern Collegiate Baseball League, Valley Baseball League and the Cape Cod Baseball League.

Having been in existence over one hundred years the Cape Cod League serves as the grandfather of all summer collegiate leagues. Its list of alumni is a who's who of Major League Baseball. In 2007 one out of every seven major league players spent at least one summer on the Cape. With its attractive setting beyond the Sagamore Bridge the CCBL consists of ten teams: the Bourne Braves, Brewster Whitecaps, Chatham Athletics, Cottuit Kettleers, Falmouth Commodores, Harwich Mariners, Hyannis Mets, Orleans Cardinals, Wareham Gate-men and 2007 league champion, the Yarmouth-Dennis Red Sox.

The Valley League boasts its own impressive list of players that have moved on to the pro ranks including the Cubs' Juan Pierre and Boston's Mike Lowell. The Valley's 2007 roster includes the Covington Lumberjacks, Fauquier Gators, playing in Bing Crosby Stadium - the Front Royal Cardinals, the Harrisonburg Turks, Haymarket Senators, Luray Wranglers, New Market Rebels, Staunton Braves, Winchester Royals, Woodstock River Bandits and league champ, the Waynesboro Generals.

Nick Swisher, Paul Quantrill, and Dave Dellucci all spent time in the Great Lakes League. Sporting some of the best team logos in summer ball the Great Lakes league includes the Anderson Servants, Cincinnati Steam, Columbus All-Americans, Delaware Cows, Grand Lake Mariners, Lake Erie Monarchs, Licking County Settlers, Lima Locos, Southern Ohio Copperheads, Stark County Terriers and the Xenia Athletes in Action.

The Atlantic Collegiate Baseball League's Wolff Division consists of the Jersey Pilots, Kutztown Rockies, Lehigh Valley Katz, and the Quakertown Blazers. The Long Island Mustangs, Metro NY Cadets, New York Generals and Stamford Robins make up the ACBL's Kaiser Division.

Playing under the lights of Tropicana Field the Leesburg Lightning captured the 2007 Florida League title by knocking off the Altamonte Springs Snappers. The Sanford River Rats, Winter Springs Barracudas, Orlando Hammers and Winter Park Diamond Dawgs round out the remainder of the league.

The Morganton Aggies outlasted the Ashville Redbirds to win the 2007 Southern League Jeffers Cup. The two combatants outlasted the Carolina Chaos, Carolina Sox, Davidson Copperheads, Monroe Channelcats, Spartanburg Crickets and the Tennessee Tornado.

Last but not least, the DuBois Bombers captured the four-team Central Illinois Collegiate League title. The Bombers battled the DuPage Dragons, Quincy Gems and Danville Dans for the crown.

Eleven current major leaguers have called the NYCBL home for at least one season. Tim Hudson, the Atlanta Braves' ace, played with Hornell in 1996. That same year Houston's Brad Lidge tossed heat for the Ithaca Lakers. Notre Dame selected Lidge in the first round of the '98 draft. Four years previous San Francisco's Steve Kline helped Little Falls to the NYCBL title. The following year, 1993, Toronto's John McDonald played for the Cohocton Red Wings. It was McDonald who was fooled into allowing a pop-up in the infield to drop when Alex Rodriguez ran by and called for the ball.

San Diego's Scott Cassidy helped the Geneva Knights to the '98 league title while St. Louis's Josh Kinney pitched for Hornell during that same summer. One season later, Tampa Bay's Brendan Harris played for the

Schenectady (now Amsterdam) Mohawks. Pittsburgh's Rajai Davis led Hornell to the 2000 league title. In 2002, Houston's Hunter Pence played for Schenectady while Toronto's Jeremy Accardo pitched for the Wellsville (now Allegany County) Nitros. Oakland's Dallas Braden pitched for Hornell in 2003.

Current minor leaguers Lou Merloni, Terry Tiffee, Scott Sauerbeck, Brad Hassey, Val Pascucci, Earl Snyder and Brett Carroll have all spent time playing summer ball in upstate New York along with retired major leaguers Kirt Manwaring, Clay Bellinger, Archi Cianfrooco, Glen Barker, Tim Naehring and Greg LaRocca.

Fourteen teams in two divisions comprise the 2007 NYCBL lineup. The Glens Falls Golden Eagles, Saratoga Phillies, Watertown Wizards, Little Falls Miners, Amsterdam Mohawks and Bennington Bombers make up the East Division while the Elmira Pioneers, Geneva Red Wings, Allegany County Nitros, Hornell Dodgers, Brockport Riverbats, Webster Yankees and Bolivar A's do battle in the West Division.

The league mixes a group of hard-working owners, coaches and managers with a bit of nostalgia. For instance, the Pioneers of Elmira play in Dunn Field. The classic stadium, featuring a covered grandstand, opened in 1939 and hosted a team with the same name for decades in the New York-Penn (NY-P) League. The Pios boast one of the league's more memorable mascots.

Complete with coonskin cap and buckskin pants, "Stitches," is a fan favorite. The happy baseball can be seen boppin' through the Dunn Field grandstand.

In Geneva, Dave Herbst turned away the wrecking ball and saved McDonough Park. After hosting the NY-P action of the Geneva Red Legs and Cubs for four decades, the grand old park at the end of Lyceum Street sat dormant and plans were made to level the stadium that opened in 1958. Then, Herbst came along and serving as owner, general manager, head coach, chief cook and bottle washer he saved baseball along the shores of Seneca Lake. Herbst is unashamed to admit that the first year of existence was a little rough. "We didn't have enough money to pay for water or electricity. When we returned from away games, I would have to give my guys flashlights, so they could find their way around the clubhouse."

Five years later, with the support of Senator Nozzolio and aggressive promotions, the Red Wings hope to turn a profit. McDonough Park now sports a brand-new deck complete with Adirondack lounge chairs available for early arrivers. A covered picnic area along the right field line makes for a great spot to entertain large groups such as the DeSales High School class of '82 reunion.

Just minutes from one of the Natural Wonders of the World, Sal Maglie field in Niagara Falls hosts the NYCBL's Power. Nestled in the quaint Hyde Park section of town, the facility also serves as home to the University of Niagara. Children can be heard frantically scrambling for foul balls, so they can receive a piece of candy in exchange from the concession stand. One of the local eateries, Porky's, advertises as "The Best Food In Foul Territory."

Positioned in the center of town, Hornell's Maple City Park is a hub of activity. A message board greets visitors at the gate with the night's starting lineup. Built in the '60's Maple City has a cozy grandstand with great sight lines.

At Amsterdam's Shuttleworth Park folks can take in the sights and sounds of a ball game. Kids participate in the annual "best Mohawk" haircut contest. Shuttleworth hosted the 2007 NYCBL All-Star game.

Duffy Fairgrounds is home to the Watertown Wizards. Found near Coffeen Street off Route 81 the sixty-seven acre area serves as a recreational area for residents. John McGraw, NYCBL's director of media relations, can be heard calling the Wizards' play-by-play.

John Mayotte won his 100th NYCBL game coaching the 2007 East-Division Champion Glens Falls Eagles. The Eagles call East Field Stadium their home.

In 1996, the league was known as Northeast Collegiate Baseball. Ed Daub served as commissioner. The 1994 MLB work stoppage and new collective bargaining agreement reduced the league funding from $35,000 to

$5,000. At the end of the season, Daub took a position with the Cincinnati Reds. Tom Kenney, then general manager of the Hornell Dodgers, approached the recently retired H. David Chamberlain about the vacancy. Kenney could think of no one better to lead the league into the twenty-first century than the coach who took the MCC program from its infancy to the point of being a perennial national junior college contender.

Chamberlain started the Monroe Community College program in 1964 when then athletic director, Gene Monaghan appointed the native of Ovid, New York as head coach. He started with $500. Thirty-three seasons later, Chamberlain amassed a record of 735 wins and 232 losses. Under his watchful eye, Tribune teams won ten Regional Championships and made two Junior College World Series appearances. Along the way, fifty MCC Tribunes were selected in the Major League draft, and countless others moved on to four-year schools.

When Kenney approached Chamberlain, the recently retired coach was ecstatic. He told his wife: "This will be great. The season is only two months long. I can play golf in the day and go watch some baseball at night." Little did the coach realize what he had ahead of him.

Chamberlain took charge from there. Eight teams competed in one division. Major League Baseball offered $5,000 worth of support, and teams supplied their own umpires. Ten years later, the league changed its name to better suit the locale, MLB has gradually upped its funding to $40,000, a union of umpires works the league, and the NYCBL has expanded to fourteen teams. Chamberlain continues to succeed, and because of that, owners and general re-elect him each year.

Knowing that people have to be part of the results Chamberlain has set an example to be followed. Nothing gets overlooked beginning with baseballs used in every game. Each team is supplied two dozen baseballs by the league. Baseballs can cost up to $50 per dozen. With Chamberlain's hard work and reputation the NYCBL has secured a contract with Diamond baseballs at a rate of $27.50 per box, a savings of over $500 per team.

With the same spirit of thrift and efficiency, Chamberlain brokered contracts with D-Bat and Pro-Line. Having each player in the league choose from bats with similar specifications creates a balance of competition. It also creates a savings for each team. D-Bat also rewards the teams with complimentary fungoes and souvenir bats to sell. Teams also receive a group rate on individual hats provided by Pro-Line. A hat that would carry a twenty dollar retail price costs the league nine dollars each. Pro-Line includes the team logo design and setup in the price.

The NYCBL is the only summer collegiate league to hold its own scout day. Scheduled around the league all-star game, the event brings together players, coaches and professional scouts. With each major league team represented, players have the opportunity not only to perform for scouts but also to receive constructive feedback.

When taking over Chamberlain needed to deal with the touchy subject of umpires. Prior to his arrival, teams scheduled their own umpiring crews. Impartiality and competition suffered. The new commissioner quickly contracted the American Baseball Umpires' Association (ABUA), and an improved product on the field resulted.

Chamberlain's efforts increased funding the NYCBL receives from MLB. When he attends the annual national meeting, the commissioner provides Major League Baseball representatives with an ever-improving portfolio. The league has increased its number of former players in the professional baseball. Competition and attendance have improved. That translates into MLB wanting to promote the league.

Chamberlain continues to look to future improvements. One idea is a possible all-star game between the NYCBL and the ACBL.   Along with Atlantic commissioner, Tom Bonekemper, Chamberlain hopes to iron out the details and schedule an event at either Shea or Yankee Stadium.

Further, the commissioner wants to try crossover games between the two divisions. He understands the challenges presented with such a proposition. Travel necessitates increased funding. Players need lodging provided when playing a night game three to four hours from home.

All these ideas keep the commissioner busy. Chamberlain continues to receive the vote of the league leaders. The commissioner keeps developing a league where guys like "Moonlight" Graham can come and spend a summer; a league where on any given night a passersby can catch a glimpse of something special. Like that familiar restaurant that one frequents, the NYCBL's charm assures return visits from fans.

Chapter 5

Change in the Air

After the loss to Niagara, Kelly knew something had to be done. His team was too good to be four and eleven. Changes were needed, but the coach understood the delicate balance of a team. Switching a player to a new defensive position or to a new spot in the batting order can trigger a domino effect. Moving a player in the batting order was tricky. A kid moving up might take advantage of the opportunity. He also might feel a pressure to perform. Then, one must consider the player who is being replaced, and the feelings of self-doubt that occur.

While all these considerations are understood when playing for a team, Kelly knew change can elicit a variety of responses; it can have a polarizing effect. Some enjoy the variety offered and find refreshment in a new perspective. Others bristle at the thought, thinking that change for the sake of change is irresponsible. Many don't like the thought of being uprooted from a comfort zone. Perhaps the most telling description of change can be found in the paradox - the only constant is change.

Change for an individual can be difficult, even painful; it usually comes after a lengthy period of self-reflection and recognition of needed improvement. Within a group it can create fear and anxiety. For a team, change can be threatening.

When dealing with a young American male, the subject of change can be even more overwhelming. Young males take pride in their accomplishments and abilities. They tend to suppress any feelings of hurt or sadness. For Mike Kelly and the Webster Yankees, making adjustments required careful consideration. Rosters froze after the all-star break. Kelly wanted to avoid alienating any of the troops.

On June twenty-sixth, Webster entered play with a record of four wins and twelve losses. Adjustments were needed. Brust, the ever-wise one, had been chirping in Kelly's ear. Those suggestions started to take hold. It was as if Kelly was playing Yahtzee and after his first roll, he decided he needed a new perspective. He returned all five dice to the tumbler to see what he could get.

During batting practice that night, Brust spent time rapping fungoes to Santos at third. With a protective screen in front of the bag while his teammates took turns inside the turtle, Santos reacquainted himself with the left side of the infield. He spent most of his career playing shortstop. He earned first-team All-District in 2006 playing short at Monroe before moving on to North Carolina A & T. There Santos settled into third base. After a hectic fall schedule full of intra-squad scrimmages followed by a fifty-nine game spring schedule, Santos experienced a dead arm feeling. He returned to New York needing a break from throwing the ball across the infield every day. Kelly agreed.

Through fifteen games, Santos played first, second and designated hitter. Five different teammates manned the hot corner. The results lacked encouragement: nineteen errors made by the infield and only six double plays turned. Worst yet, the infield lacked aggressiveness and cohesion. The unit could not be counted on to make a big play.

Playing at third created a metamorphosis. Santos's body language changed. Rather than fielding balls back on his heels, the infielder regained his aggressive hands. His shoulders leaned forward, and his deft footwork returned.

Moving Santos to third opened up first base for McIntyre. Having four catchers Kelly needed to rotate the backstops through and keep them fresh. That meant using one of the catchers as a designated hitter. McIntyre's bat was too good to leave out of the lineup, but outfield did not seem like the position for the young hitter. With Santos playing third, McIntyre fit at first. One part of the lineup took shape.

Helmick settled in at second; a position where he seemed more comfortable. Bertolini took over at short – a spot that allowed his leadership talents to grow.

The second sign of change came when Brown eagerly inquired about the online broadcast of games. He wanted his parents to listen to the June twenty-seventh game against Elmira because he was getting the start. For Brown the season had been as up and down as the Jack Rabbit roller coaster ride at nearby Sea Breeze Park. The Annapolis, Maryland native pitched to three batters in the season's second game. He struck out the side in order. Niagara hitters couldn't catch his heat, and Brown's dirty deuce left Power batters swinging from their front foot. Against Bolivar on June 20th, he allowed no runs while striking out two in two innings of work. Again, everything was working for Brown.

Beyond those relief appearances, Brown struggled. He entered the game against the Elmira Pioneers with an earned run average of 7.71.

There was the third game of the year. Encouraged by the previous night's performance, Kelly went back to the young reliever. This time, he surrendered five hits and two runs striking out none in one inning of work. Three days later, he walked three of the eight batters he faced. His second appearance against Niagara resembled nothing of the first outing. In three and two-thirds, he walked three, hit two, gave up three hits, and two of the four runs he allowed were earned. Against Allegany County, he faced five batters and allowed two runs.

Putting Brown in the starting rotation had Brust written all over it. Only the ex-pro could surmise that the chance was worth taking. Brown struggled coming out of the bullpen. The first batter or two he faced caused problems. Then he tightened. Giving him a start could put his mind at ease. He would get a chance to prove himself in a longer outing.

The move meant someone needed to go to the bullpen. Kelly established and wanted to keep a consistent rotation. "Bomber" made the change. He provided insurance as a long reliever, and Kelly wanted to increase the number of Curynski's outings.

Brown proved to be the elixir that Webster needed. He limited the Pio's to two runs and left with the lead and two out in the sixth. Curynski came on and retired the side with one pitch. "Bomber" gave up a run in the seventh. Bernath allowed a run in the eighth. Gardner struck out four of the five he faced. In the ninth, he spit nine seeds and struck out the side.

The win ended a six-game slide and put some giddy-up in the gait of the Yanks. While the infield did not turn any double plays, the presence of Santos at third was having a profound effect. Now in his third game at the corner, bunts that were getting in for singles turned into routine outs. Swinging bunts – when a batter takes a full swing, makes partial contact only to have the ball travel the distance of a bunt – caused little problem for Santos as he gracefully gathered and threw the ball in one smooth motion. The hole between third and short was shored up, and Bertolini relaxed. McIntyre took extra fungoes at first, and Helmick looked at ease playing second.

The following day, Webster returned to their opening day location, Brockport. After the recent drubbing by the Riverbats, this game made for a potential disaster. Any momentum recently gained could be stymied by the cross-town rival.

Instead, Webster rolled the tide. The Yanks rallied to tie the game at two in the seventh. Stuckless led off with a single and eventually scored on McIntyre's two-out base hit to right. Veenema scattered eight hits over seven and a third. The lefty exited the game in the eighth after experiencing tightness in his shoulder while making a diving catch on a pop-up bunt. Coleman was pressed into service. He retired the side, but not without some dramatics. With one out and a runner on third a sinking line drive into right seemed destined to score the leading run. That is until Sullivan made a shoestring catch and air mailed the ball to "KB" for the tag at home.

Gardner retired the side in the ninth and tenth when the game went extra innings. In the eleventh, Webster erupted for seven runs off Davis-Brockport's starter when the Riverbats pummeled the Yanks. Bertolini and Stuckless led off with back-to-back singles before Bailey reached on an error. Santos delivered two with a one-hop double off the fence in left center. After an intentional walk to McIntyre, a couple of sac flies and a pair of Brockport errors, Bertolini finished the scoring with a bases-loaded double.

For Bertolini, the extra-frame was especially satisfying. The infielder came into the game with four hits in forty-six at bats. "Finally!" said Bertolini of his leadoff single. "It was a fastball in. I hope to keep this going."

Bernath retired the side in the eleventh. Webster 9 Brockport 2.

Brown's name did not appear in the box score, but he affected the outcome of the game. The previous day's outing put a little swagger back in his step. Against Brockport, it was his suggestion to play "pick to click"- a game usually reserved for the pitchers not in the game. The rules are rather simple: each reserve player picks a teammate as his player for the day. That player can earn a point for a single, a run scored or an RBI. Doubles fetch a deuce; triples get the trifecta. Yard work grabs a six pack. A player can lose points for a whiff or an error.

Brown grabbed pen and pad and completed the ledger. Bobby D., as shy as a Times Square hooker, took McIntyre right away. Brown followed and chose Santos. Carmody went with Stucky. Bernath took Helmick. Coleman opted for Lawler. Bertolini, who started the game on the bench, weighed in on Bailey.

Chatter returned to the dugout. Guys started cheering for each other. The talk was all baseball.

At one point the topic of a double play arises. Should a player lose points? Stifler, the bullpen catcher for the day, happened to be in the dugout at this point. "You can't lose points on a DP. What if it's a line drive? And the base runner makes the mistake."

To reinforce Stiffy's logic players exchange stories of base-running gaffes witnessed.

Gino, showing his baseball encyclopedia of knowledge, referred to the infamous play known as "Merkle's Boner." In 1908, Fred Merkle, then playing for the New York Giants, cost his team the pennant when he failed to touch second base to avoid the crush of zealous fans pouring onto the field.

The mood became infectious. Contestants in "pick to click" couldn't help paying attention to each at bat. The excitement grew with each trip to the plate. When Joey McIntyre drove home the tying run with a single, DiNuzzo jumped out of the dugout clapping and cheering. Little did he know Stucky's run contributed to the seven points accumulated on the day. No one will approach that number. At that moment it doesn't matter; McIntyre has earned Bobby D. two points.

They have known each other for little more than three weeks, brought together by the common language of baseball. Sights, sounds and nuances are all familiar. Today the team bonded. Cohesion took place. A simple game such as "pick to click," added to the other commonalities, created an emotional attachment between young men who were becoming brothers.

In the fifth, Helmick was tagged out at home and landed awkwardly on his already tender right ankle. He tried to walk it off. When it appeared to be no use, Helmick begged out, and Bertolini entered the game. It was DiNuzzo at this point who volunteered to wrap Helmick's ankle. The gesture seemed basic, but three weeks ago DiNuzzo was a kid from Rockland County, New York, and Helmick a kid from Severn, Maryland. Today, DiNuzzo showed concern for Helmick. Today, they are teammates.

Like Pullyblank, Brown experienced his own detour. Growing up in Maryland, he had the good fortune in high school of working under the tutelage of Clayton Jacobsen of the Baltimore Orioles. At an early age, he learned the proper mechanics associated with his arm slot and follow-through. Then he played for the Maryland Orioles of the Cal Ripken Sr. League. One year ago he pitched for the Waynesboro Generals of the Valley, a second tier summer league. He seemed on pace for a career in baseball. That is until he became academically ineligible. Instead of continuing on the path set out, Brown sat and watched as his Towson University teammates played their 2007 season in the Colonial Athletic Association. For now, Brown seemed to have found his path again.

The game against Brockport meant something more for Veenema, Gardner and Adam Perlo. Two nights prior five recent graduates of Fairport High School died in an automobile accident. The tragedy tore a hole through the tight-knit community. Vigils took place. Memorials were held. While Veenema, Gardner and Perlo knew none of the victims personally, the incident brought the fragile nature of life into plain view. All three graduated from Fairport High School. Gardner went through school with one of the victims' brother. Veenema was good friends with the brother of another. Perlo attended all of the funerals. The three donned arm bands for the remainder of the season. Veenema inscribed the initials of the fallen on the band of his hat. After Gardner's warm-up tosses, he drew the number five in the dirt on the back of the mound. All wanted to show their support for the community.

Momentum continued to build for Webster. DiNuzzo took the hill as the Yanks faced Niagara the following night. Bobby D. put the Brockport debacle behind him. He limited the Power to no runs on three hits through seven. Bobby D. left the Power hitters mumbling and shaking their heads.

In the eighth, Niagara touched Bobby D. for two runs on three hits, but by that time the Webster bats scored five. When DiNuzzo retired the final batter in the eighth on strikes, he bounced from the mound, pumped his fist and let out a burst of emotion. The season was starting to mean something.

DiNuzzo turned the tables on his fate. In his previous two appearances opponents earned Player-Of-The-Day Honors. Eric Ferguson set an NYCBL record with seven runs batted in. Doug Cialella pitched a complete game shutout. This time it was Bobby D.'s turn for the honors as he earned Player-Of-The-Day.

Curynski struck out two of the three he faced in the ninth to pick up the save. Webster 5 Niagara 2.

Offerman took the ball the following afternoon against Hornell. Gino held the Dodgers to three runs over seven innings. Bernath pitched a scoreless eighth. Gardner picked up the save, striking out one in the ninth. Once again, Webster bats strung together hits. "KB" and Johnson scored on Sullivan's one-out triple in the third. Sullivan scored when Bertolini's ground ball was booted in the infield. Lawler led the sixth with a bunt single. He stole second, advanced to third on Johnson's fly ball and scored the eventual winning run on a wild pitch.

Lawler's play symbolized the new-found Webster enthusiasm. Having rapped a pair of round trippers early in the season along with several doubles – including the walk-off double to beat Bolivar-the young hitter found himself mired in a slump. Instead of trying to swing his way out, Lawler chose to manufacture a run. After the game, the young hitter commented, "I've been struggling. I needed to do something to contribute."

Webster found their groove – for the fourth consecutive game the starting pitcher worked at least six strong innings. Like clockwork, the bullpen closed the game. Hits came in bunches. For the second day in a row, the infield turned a double play. Curynski gave the bullpen a second stopper. Kelly wouldn't have to worry about overworking Gardner.

With the win, Webster improved to eight wins and twelve losses and moved to within four games of the playoffs. Plenty of time remained to make up ground and to test the mettle of this new-found team.

The following night Webster travelled to Scio and squared off with first-place Allegany County. The Nitros were red-hot, winning their last eight and seventeen of eighteen. Before Carmody took the mound, an ominous event occurred. Santos, the second batter of the game, drilled a deep fly to the opposite field. Like any outfielder is taught, the Nitro player found the fence with his hand and leapt to stab the pearl from the air. As the Nitro right-fielder pushed the section of fence, it collapsed allowing him to catch a ball that would have otherwise landed for a home run. Instead of a one-run lead, Webster took the field tied at zero.

Two of four Nitro runs for the game came as the result of errors made in right field. Allegany County won its ninth in a row, four to three.

The loss was particularly frustrating for Carmody as he scattered seven hits over six innings striking out three and walking two. For the second consecutive outing, he gave his team a chance to win. Instead, he took the loss. He seemed harassed by bad fortune. Tonight, the freak occurrence in right field cost his team a run in the first, and then two errors contributed to half the Nitro output.

Webster went to Hornell the next day to play the fourth-place Dodgers. Responding to the loss would be an important test of the team's resolve. The four-game winning streak offered a shot of adrenalin. But adrenalin is for sprints. Baseball is a marathon.

As the setting sun glared into the first base dugout Gino commented: "It's like a bible thing; you have to go through the desert before you get to the "promised land."

Early on, Webster appeared ready to respond. Helmick led off the game with a single and scored one-out later on a Santos single. After a wild pitch allowed Nelson to move up to second, McIntyre followed with a double, and Webster led two-zip. Brown pitched out of a jam in the bottom of the stanza limiting the Dodgers to one run.

Webster scored a run in the third. Bailey tripled to get things started. Santos followed with an RBI single. Two Dodger errors helped in the fourth as Bertolini and Gardner – showing his versatility and playing in right field- scored. Lawler and Sullivan crossed the dish in the fifth, and Webster led seven to one.

Brown stumbled in the bottom of the inning. Before Curynski entered and retired the first batter he faced to end the inning, Hornell scored four runs on four hits. Despite the damage done, Webster still led. With "Bomber" on the hill, spirits remained aloft.

Hornell failed to get a ball out of the infield in the sixth. Curynski gave up a leadoff walk in the seventh but erased the runner with a double play. After going 0 and 2, the next batter shortened his swing and fouled away a pair of pitches. Curynski, in complete command, delivered another heater. The batter merely put the barrel of the bat on the ball and let the pitch's velocity do the work. The ball landed on the outfield grass just past Helmick's outstretched glove. Then the unimaginable – "Bomber" bounced a slider in front of the plate, and the runner moved to second. Again, the batter shortened his swing on a two-strike count, made contact, and the runner scored. Webster 7 Hornell 6.

Curynski fanned two in the eighth. Gardner made a bee line from right field to the bullpen, donned a hoodie and began to warm up. He skipped the sprints because he did plenty throughout the game running from the dugout to the field. First, he worked the stretch cords, then came the towel-to reinforce his reach to the plate, next a green, nine-ounce ball for a few tosses before he toes the bullpen rubber. "Stiffy" set in the crouch. Ten fast balls, three curves, three change, fast ball, curve, change, change, curve and finish with the heat. Gardner was ready. Lawler was stranded at third. Three outs to victory.

Three pitches – one out. Gardner went 0 and 2 on the next batter before a broken-bat single landed limply in the right-field grass. It was not a problem. Webster had the lead. They focused on the batter.

Then, for whatever reason, Gardner expe-rienced a momentary lapse of reason. He had been dominating batters since the Brockport debacle. He struck out seven consecutive at one point. Maybe, the fact that tonight he played in the field dulled his senses just enough to matter. Maybe, the late hour affected him. Perhaps, the cool valley air at night caused a distraction. Whatever the cause, the effect was improbable.

Gardner's snap throw to first kicked in the dirt through McIntyre's legs and into foul territory. Had it been any other diamond in the league, the ball would have caromed off the fence a few feet away. But the foul territory at Maple City Park extends well over a hundred feet past the dugout and beyond the bullpen. By the time McIntyre retrieved the errant throw, the tying run stood ninety feet away from home plate. The batter lifted a fly ball to right field - a can of corn, but no chance for a play at the plate.

Webster's six-run lead evaporated. They were two outs away from gaining ground in the playoff race. They were two outs from getting home before midnight. Now the game was up for grabs.

The teams traded jabs for two innings. Hornell loaded the bases on three walks in the tenth, but Bernath induced a ground ball for the final out. Kelly might need DiNuzzo to toss an inning. Bobby D. grabbed his bag and found his spikes. For the second time in a week, Sullivan made a throw from right field to catch a runner at the plate. This time it was a relay through Helmick. DiNuzzo did not have enough time to change shoes. He still had a sneaker on one foot, and a cleat halfway on the other as he led the rush onto the field to congratulate his teammates. All follow and congregated around Helmick and Sullivan.

Sullivan rapped a one-out single in the twelfth and advanced to second on an error. Webster was one hit away from the lead as Bertolini, the extra-inning hero at Brockport, walked to the plate.

At five feet, nine inches Bertolini is a tower of energy and enthusiasm. He is the first one to lend a hand taking care of the infield. The scrappy infielder is the Maytag Man's favorite player because he never leaves the field of play with a clean uniform. Any runner at second base is subjected to a series of feints and dodges as Bertolini attempts to hold the runner and fill the hole at short.

He worked the count full. Finally, he got a pitch he could hit and sent a flair into right center. Sullivan took off on contact. With the ball sinking, Kelly waved Sullivan home. Then, the speedy Hornell center-fielder, Philip Brewington Jr., appeared out of nowhere and made a diving stab. Sullivan was around third and had no chance. Threat extinguished. Hornell scored in the bottom of the inning and won eight to seven.

With clouds of second guessing swirling round their heads the Webster Yankees left Hornell and headed north on Route 390. They had fallen five games back of the playoff race. The late finish of the night's game didn't bode well for the next day's 1p.m. start against Bolivar.

Webster could have relied on a litany of excuses for a poor outing against the A's. The baseball gods seemed evil of late. Tantalized by a four-game win streak the Yankees looked like a team of destiny. It appeared that any bump in the road could be overcome.

Suddenly, everything changed. Victory seemed elusive. A sure home run removed by a collapsing fence. Two errors in right field and a wild pickoff at first at the only stadium known to mankind where there is enough room for the tying run to advance from first to third. Webster seemed to experience more than their fair share of freak occurrences.

Webster had one game remaining before the all-star break. Knowing that his players wouldn't get home before one in the morning, Kelly cancelled the batting practice. Rest was important. A loss to Bolivar would linger for three days. Bolivar, with a record of three wins and nineteen losses, stared up at the rest of the NYCBL West Division. Two days ago Webster looked poised to make a run at the playoffs. Two one-run losses left the Yanks downtrodden.

Kelly had every right to be concerned about the fragile psyche of the team. Beating Bolivar seemed paramount.

Instead of an exercise in self-pity, Webster responded with a rousing victory, 7-3. Veenema limited Bolivar hitters to six hits and two runs while striking out five and walking two. Coleman gave up a run on two hits over two innings. Gardner returned to form retiring all three batters he faced in the ninth.

Gardner's performance showed his true competitive fire. Little more than fifteen hours after his broken pickoff at first the southpaw took the mound with an air of dogged determination. He fanned the first batter he faced. The second broke his bat and weakly popped up to Bertolini. The final batter hit a lazy fly to shallow center. One-half of the season was behind them, and Gardner had not allowed an extra-base hit.

McIntyre and Johnson led a fifteen-hit attack. Two of McIntyre's three hits on the day go for doubles. He drove in two and is on base when Lawler goes deep.

Johnson roped a double, three singles, scored one and drove in two.

Helmick, Perlo and Bertolini all chipped in two hits apiece.

Webster's record stood at nine wins and fourteen losses - the playoffs three games away. McIntyre, Gardner and Stuckless headed to Shuttleworth Park in Amsterdam for the all-star game. McIntyre earned the NYCBL West Division Player-of-the-Week. During the week of the four- game win streak he batted .478 with four runs batted in, three runs scored, and five consecutive multi-hit games.

Gardner elicited a few "ooohs" and "ahhhhs" when his heat registered 92 on the Jugs guns of a few MLB scouts sitting behind home plate at Shuttleworth. Stucky hit a frozen rope single.

DiNuzzo, "KB" and Gino hung around Rochester for the break. Nineteen games remained. Change had been a good thing.

Danny Bertolini with Shawn Bailey in the background

Shawn Bailey

Joe McIntyre with the stretch

Bobby D.

Nelson Santos

Ryan Sullivan

Kevin Carmody

"KB" getting the truth from Brusty

Gino

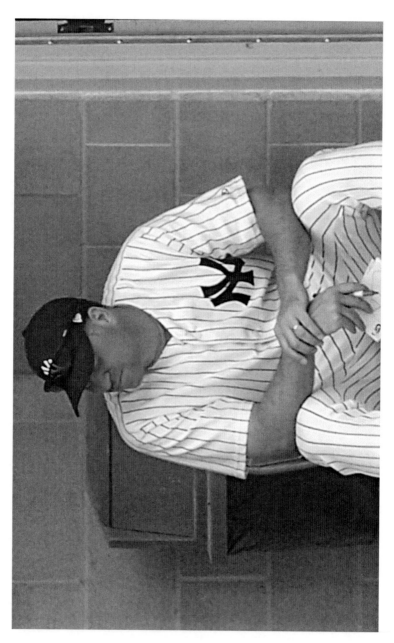

Brusty

Mark Perlo

Mike Kelly

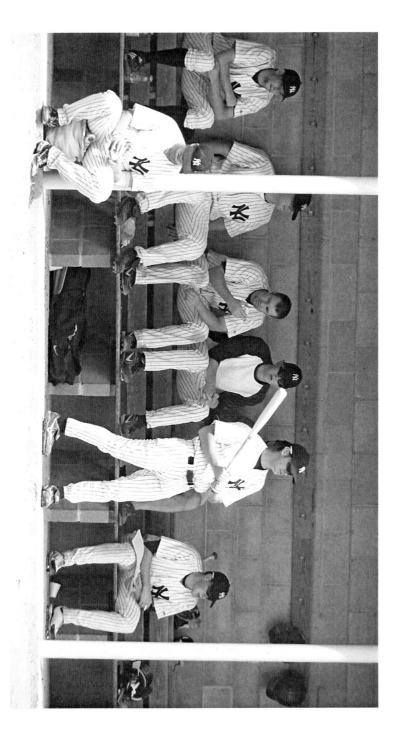

NATIONAL ALLIANCE OF COLLEGE SUMMER BASEBALL

White: Summer
Baseball
Clearinghouse
Yellow: League
Commissioner
Pink: Team

2010 Letter of Commitment

Name of League __New York Collegiate League__ Date Issued _____

(To be signed within 21 days)

Team _____

Name of Player _____ Date of Birth _____

Home Address _____ City _____ State _____ Zip _____

E-Mail _____ Home Telephone (_____) _____

Player Cell Phone (_____) _____

College (Spring 2009) _____ Year in School (Spring 2009) ___1___ 2 ___3

(Circle One)

Campus Mailing Address _____ City _____ State _____ Zip _____

☐ Please check this box if you wish to be employed during the 2009 summer league session. A LEAGUE IS NOT REQUIRED TO secure employment for you; however, by indicating your interest in employment, league representatives will be able to assist you better.

☐ Please check this box if you wish to live with a host family during the summer league season. Host Families may be a requirement in some summer collegiate wood bat leagues in the NACSB

Attention

- It is important to read this entire document carefully before signing this letter of commitment, since it is mandatory for all student-athletes playing in an NACSB-sanctioned summer baseball league.
- By signing this agreement, I certify that I will not use any form of tobacco during practice sessions or contests.

I understand that by signing this document I am committed to the above team and to the league, which is an NACSB-sanctioned summer baseball league.

I am also committed to abiding by the specific league's and team's code of conduct manual and their rules and regulations. I have not signed, and will not sign, any other commitment form for the designated season. Signing this document prohibits me from participating on any other summer league team. I may participate on other outside teams only according to team and league regulations.

I understand that this is a direct offer of the team to fill a place on its team roster in accordance with these rules of the league.

I understand that I may be released from this letter of commitment only in the event of my signing a professional contract; being selected to an active traveling all-star team sanctioned by or sponsored by the NCAA, NJCAA, NAIA, and the U.S. Olympic Committee or any of its subordinate committees, or a similar amateur athletics authority; or by written mutual consent of the commissioner of both involved leagues. I understand that I may be released from this commitment by the team and/or league specified above if I am deemed injured and unable to perform.

I understand that this letter of commitment is not valid until each of the requested signatures is obtained.

Player's Signature _____ Date _____

Athletics Director's (or official representative) signature _____ Date _____

Team/League's Signature _____ Date _____

NACSB Member Leagues - Atlantic Collegiate Baseball League, Cape Cod Baseball League, Central Illinois Collegiate League, Florida Collegiate Summer League, Great Lakes Summer Collegiate League, New York Collegiate Baseball League, Southern Collegiate Baseball League, Valley Baseball League.

Chapter 6

Mike Kelly

Time spent in the dugout near Mike Kelly can be an exercise in unintentional enlightenment. With the diamond as his sanctuary and dugout as his pulpit, the thirty-something freely expounds on the world around him. "Buckle your seat belts when you're around me," frequently cautions the young coach.

Amid his mini-rants on music, politics, American education and the take-out meal from last night, Kelly reveals much of his character in one statement: "Sympathy is only found in the dictionary." It takes little to get Kelly to clarify this motto. "Yeah, and it's somewhere between shithead and syphilis."

As simple as it may appear, this mantra provides a glimpse inside a young coach who, if he has learned nothing else, has learned an appreciation for everything he has.

It is no coincidence that Michael Kelly came into the world on August fifth, 1977 to Mary and Mike Kelly Sr. in the city of Allentown, Pennsylvania - the city romanticized by Billy Joel for its hard work and misfortune as jobs left town.

The family moved soon after with the father's new job and lived in Fort Washington, D.C. until 1981. Mike Sr. worked retail for the Woolco Corporation. Mike Jr.'s one memory of his time spent near the nation's capital being Redskins' day at school when his mother made a stop at a 7-Eleven to make sure her son had a hat for the day.

Woolco transferred the elder Kelly to Detford, New Jersey, and the family moved. There Mike's younger sister, Megan, was born. Soon after, Woolco went out of business.

With his experience in retail and merchandising Mike Sr. took a chance on a growing, western New York grocery store named Wegmans. The hunch paid off as two decades later the family-owned store was a regular in Fortune 500 magazine. While at one time stores were limited to the Rochester area, now they stretch along the eastern sea board. So engrained in the local fabric is Wegmans that a home's value can be directly related to its driving distance from the nearest Wegmans location.

Originally, Mike Sr. worked at the East Avenue store. The family settled nearby, and Mike Jr. attended St. John's, Humboldt Street on the city's south east side.

The family grew by one when Matthew came into the world.

When Mike Jr. was in third grade, Mike Sr. took a job at the Driving Park Avenue Wegmans, and the family moved cross-town and settled on Augustine St. in a second-floor apartment above Mary's parents.

The community settled in, known as the Tenth Ward or otherwise, Maplewood, stretches to its natural boundary on the east being the Genesee River with its picturesque gorge that draws throngs of photographers each fall looking to capture the bounty of changing leaf colors.

To the west Mount Read Boulevard separates the Tenth Ward from its neighboring suburbs of Greece and Gates. Dewey and Lake Avenues run from Holy Sepulchre cemetery to the north and Lexington Avenue to the south.

In the 1980s, this urban neighborhood was an ant hill of activity. Kodak Park, an expansive industrial site stretching west from Lake Avenue to the neighboring suburb of Greece, reached its peak of employment as the photography giant had over 60,000 on its payroll during the 1980s. Founded in 1888, Eastman Kodak and Company occupied 1,300 acres with 170 buildings. By the turn of the 21st century, Kodak's labor force in Rochester dropped below 10,000.

Many of the 60,000 inhabited the Tenth Ward choosing to walk to and from work on a daily basis. Those employees, who lived in neighboring suburbs, nonetheless, took advantage of the retail and service industry surrounding Kodak Park.

Kodak employees, or "Dakkers," frequented the local taverns and restaurants. Eateries such as the Corfu and Peppermill restaurants and taverns like Muldoon's, the Pullman Car, Callaghan's, Casey Jones, the Loft and Romig's all thrived on the lunch and dinner crowds from Kodak - workers looking to fill their hungry bellies and whet their whistles.

But the neighborhood provided more than eating and drinking establishments. Piehler Pontiac on the corner of Lake Avenue and Ridge Road beckoned car buyers for miles with their spotlights that scanned the summer sky. Kitty corner to the car dealership was Grinnan's Grocery. Just a little stretch more up the sidewalk and one came to Anthony's Tailor Shop.

All within walking distance a person could get his or her footwear at Schmanke's shoes, purchase pharmaceuticals at Mount Drug or Sy's Pharmacy, enjoy a fountain soda at Wallace's, buy milk at Meizenzhal Dairy and get a trim at Ken's Barber Shop. One purchased tools and hardware at Dale's or Aero Hardware. Johnny Antonelli, Rochester's original major leaguer who compiled 126 wins during 12 seasons in the "Bigs," lent his name to the local Firestone dealership.

Business fluctuated on the semi-annual occasion of the Kodak bonus – a salary incentive given to all "Dakkers" as a sign of appreciation for a job-well done.

Knowing the bonus was coming, the smaller businesses planned sales to bring in added revenue.

It was a self-contained community, long before the term started being used, with proprietors on the premises to greet customers. Private business owners and their clientele were on a first name basis. If a mother or father frequented a place of business, his or her children also were also known to the owner.

It was a time of economic growth, but it was also a time when people remained in touch with their community. This area shaped Mike Kelly's character.

Living within five miles of Kodak Park Mike grew up in a neighborhood of white and blue-collar employees. Engineers and foremen lived on the same streets and attended the same churches with assembly-line workers; each respecting the other for his or her contributions.

Augustine St. rests at the top of the "Four Hills" of Raines Park – a small street that runs parallel and between Lake and Dewey Avenues. The name "Four Hills" derives from the ten degree drop as one proceeded north from Augustine to Alameda Street. There, the road plateaus for one lane before making a similar drop to Albemarle Street, then similarly going on to Seneca Parkway, and ending at Magee Avenue.

Mike walked this path everyday to and from Sacred Heart Cathedral School. During the fall and spring the jaunt along the tree-lined street was pleasant. Winter brought with it trepidation as ice and snow covered the sidewalks along the inclined road.

The first family car Mike remembers was a Chevy Celebrity. What the vehicle lacked in air conditioning and heat, it made up for with a sleek 8-Track tape player. When the economy car could no longer be relied upon, a Mercury Zephyr – with much the same description as the previous vehicle – was purchased.

Mike did the usual. He served as an altar boy at church. He tried his hand at Pop Warner football playing for the Tenth Ward Tigers, but he didn't like it much. He played CYO basketball, but always managed to roll one of his ankles. He also played 40 & 1 baseball.

Baseball came to him the easiest. Recognizing his son's talents, the elder Kelly served as coach for his son's little league teams. The native of Philadelphia always chose the Phillies for team uniforms much to the chagrin of his son whose team was the Mets. Nonetheless, the younger Kelly readily donned the little league cap perhaps out of sense of pride for his involvement with a game he was learning to love.

As time progressed, Mike's love for baseball grew. When he began playing Inter-Town baseball, Kelly Sr. bought a Dodge Ram conversion van. The spacious yet simplistic vehicle allowed the father to cart players and equipment throughout the suburbs of Rochester. It also doubled as an effective means of hauling supplies and materials for the elder Kelly's hobby – maintaining a flower garden around the family residence.

In the evening, Mike played the organized games of leagues. By day he and his friends spent their time with games of their own devise. With pals George Rose, Pat Harris, Rory and Tim Zimmer and Jason Barnhart, Mike set out for the fields behind nearby Aquinas Institute – a Catholic high school run by, at the time, Basilian priests. There, without enough players to fill out complete lineups, the group played either home run derby or two-base (their own version of sand lot baseball).

When it came time for Mike to enter high school, the family faced a tough decision. At one time, Mary Kelly worked in the cheese department at Wegmans. That was a departure from her dreams. She wanted to pursue a career in nursing. Even that had to be put off for the upbringing of a family. When Mike entered sixth grade, mom returned to school herself taking nursing classes at Monroe Community College.

With Mike Sr., the sole source of income in the house, the possibility of Mike continuing in a Catholic school seemed remote. There were bills to pay for Megan and Matt; Mike would attend John Marshall High – a public school in the Rochester City School District.

The building was familiar to Mike being just one block north of Sacred Heart, and he walked the same path along the "Four Hills." What was unfamiliar was his first experience as a minority. Marshall High, as part of the Rochester City School District, was predominantly an African-American population - the prospect of which never fazed Mike. He continued on his way attending classes and playing sports – football, basketball, and baseball. At that time the school district faced a budget crunch which limited sports' programs to varsity teams only. Kelly proved more than capable of competing at that level.

What started as a new beginning ended one year later when racial tensions in the school ended in a shooting between teammates on the basketball team. The school evacuated. One of the teachers, fearing for Mike's safety, walked home with the youngster.

Mike left John Marshall never to return. Fearing for his life he refused to go back. Mary Kelly with her maternal instinct on overload refused to allow her eldest to be placed in danger.

A call was placed to Mike's grandmother, Betty Kelly, in Pennsylvania. She agreed to finance Mike's tuition at Aquinas Institute.

Mike's social transition into his new school was smoothed by the many friends who already attended AQ. His adjustment into the school's sports' program didn't go as well.

A transfer ruling caused problems forcing him to play JV baseball. At the season's end five teammates earned spots on varsity for sectionals. Mike was not among them. The next year he was cut from the basketball team, and football seemed a distant memory.

His remaining years in high school seemed to only feed his appetite for baseball. He played third base for AQ but sensed there was much more to the game.

That sense led Mike to the campus of MCC. His college decision needed very little consideration. His parents asked what his favorite class was (gym) and what he wanted to do (play baseball). Mary and Mike Sr. supported their son's endeavors, and Mike enrolled.

His prospects seemed modest because Mike had at best an average high school career, and the MCC program, headed by Dave Chamberlain, realistically included on their annual list of team goals a trip to the Junior College World Series.

Mike figured the Tribune program had plenty to teach him. Little did he realize how much he would learn.

After the fall season of intra-squad scrimmages and light work outs Mike endured the grueling 6 a.m. conditioning sessions. Chamberlain used these sessions, the first of which was renowned as "hell week," as a way to weed out kids. MCC's program had grown, and with the popularity came numbers. Chamberlain needed a way to gauge the intentions of his prospects. Bringing kids in at an early hour served the purpose.

Mention "Towers" and the "six-minute mile" to any MCC baseball alum, and you'll receive a variety of responses – all colorful and with a story of woe to go along with it. Chamberlain instructed prospective players to the track on the Henrietta campus. A six-minute mile may seem modest until one considers the conditions – 6 a.m., outdoors, during the month of February in upstate New York. Those unwilling or incapable of enduring the test need not bother. All the talent in the world could not save a player from having to fulfill this requirement.

The outdoor mile was only half the battle. On opposite days players started in the gym with a variety of basic running exercises – sprints, suicides and / or "down and backs." The number of sets depended upon Chamberlain's wishes. Once completed, the athletes ran "Towers." From the gym the prospects took off through Building 10, onto Building 9 and up the eight flights of the Building 8 tower. There at the top, an assistant coach waited to take attendance. After checking in players returned to the start and began again.

The kid who knew little about air conditioning and heat in his car showed no signs of quitting. For all of his efforts and commitment, Mike was awarded the position of catcher...in the bullpen. He spent the entire season getting relief pitchers ready. He earned four at bats and managed two base hits.

He couldn't have been happier. Chamberlain showed Mike that anything worth doing was worth doing right. That hard work and commitment were the way to success. Mike also watched as Chamberlain played no favorites amongst his players. Team rules and expectations applied to everyone, and no one was above the responsibilities of the team.

It came as no surprise when Kelly earned the Coach's Award for his dedication and work ethic.

That season was Chamberlain's thirty-third and final season at the helm for MCC. One season of Chamberlain left an indelible mark on the character of Mike Kelly.

"Baseball is the most over-coached sport. You put kids out on the field, and you teach how to do the job."

Chamberlain's axiom rang in Kelly's ears.

The next season under long-time assistant Skip Bailey, Mike flourished as the starting catcher.

It was that year Mike's communication skills took shape. The position of catcher is innately unique to his teammates. The catcher being the only one facing out onto the field with the possibility of all eyes of his teammates focused upon him. He served as the conduit between coach and his battery mate and teammates. Mike, as all catchers, became responsible for delivering signs to his teammates.

"A coach can move the outfielders, but the infield hinges on the catcher. Bunt defense, third to second defense – those all come through the catcher," noted Kelly. While those signals may come from the coach, the catcher is responsible for relaying those alignments.

Kelly also learned how a catcher can affect the momentum of a game.

"A coach is limited to the number of visits to the mound, but a catcher is unlimited. Things can change rapidly for a pitcher. The catcher is usually the first person to the mound after a three-run home run. The words of a catcher can impact the outcome of the game."

Those realizations shaped Mike's perspective as he began understanding the nuances of the game. He started recognizing how the ball-strike count can dictate the pitch selection. If a pitcher missed the strike zone, by how much had it missed.

He batted over .400 that season and garnered the David Johns Memorial Award and a spot on the All-Region team.

At season's end, Mike graduated from the junior college and chose to attend nearby Brockport State. After playing two years on the campus just west of Rochester, Mike learned how much he missed the MCC way.

When he graduated from college, Kelly had one thing in mind: to once again put on the Tribune uniform.

His wish came true. He returned to the campus and worked a few camps the summer after graduating. In a case of being in the right place at the right time, Skip Bailey needed a volunteer assistant. Kelly took the job. Eventually, he took a position heading up the college's intramural program.

He completed the circle that February when he took attendance as prospects went through the paces of running "Towers." It was his first year as an assistant at Monroe Community College.

"At the end of the day we're leading them down a path, and they either take it or not. If a kid is not failing, we're not going to pull him aside. We'll let the kid fail, so they'll come to us and learn."

Chapter 7

Getting in Position

NYCBL Standings
As of July 6, 2007

Eastern	W	L	Pct.	GB
Glens Falls	19	4	.826	-
Saratoga	14	8	.636	4.5
Little Falls	9	11	.450	8.5
Watertown	9	13	.409	9.0
Bennington	7	14	.333	11.0
Amsterdam	8	16	.333	11.5

Western	W	L	Pct.	GB
Allegany Cty	21	3	.875	-
Elmira	13	10	.565	7.5
Hornell	13	11	.542	8.0
Niagara	12	11	.522	8.5
Geneva	12	13	.480	9.5
Brockport	10	11	.476	9.5
Webster	9	14	.391	11.5
Bolivar	3	20	.130	17.5

As the first half of the season ended Webster sat precariously in seventh place. On one hand, they were just three games out of the fourth and final playoff spot. On the other hand, they could smell the stench of last.

The lineup seemed in place. The rotation looked ready to go. The bullpen pecking order had been clearly established. Generating momentum stood between Webster and the "promised land" known as the playoffs.

Momentum waited for another day. Three Geneva pitchers held Webster to two hits and zero runs as the Wings topped the Yanks 4-0 to open the second half of the season.

Paul Bertuccinni earned the win as he struck out six, walked one and limited Webster to two hits through seven innings of work. Dusty Odenbach and Kyle Bellamy each tossed a perfect inning of relief. Bellamy struck out the side in the ninth for the save.

Geneva scored three runs in the third. With two outs, Brock Miller started the attack with the first of three Geneva singles. Andrew Damewood followed, and Julio Gomez drove home Miller. After a wild pitch, Damewood and Gomez both scored on a Brendan Stokes double.

DiNuzzo was looking to win his second consecutive decision. Bobby D. pitched admirably, allowing three runs over seven innings, striking out eight and walking one. Nonetheless, he took the loss.

The game was not without a little unintentional comedy. Coleman worked two innings of relief striking out two and walking one – by all estimates, a less-than-memorable performance. Except that time had to be called at one point for the umpire to inspect the young lefty's pitching hand. Coleman spent part of the all-star break enjoying some recreation by playing paint ball. The residue remaining on his hand created a distraction for opposing batters. After a brief discussion, Coleman was allowed to continue. The situation gave birth to a new nickname: "the paint ball master."

With the opportunity to win two games, the Webster offense found production from some rare sources the following night. Bertolini got hot at the plate, and Johnson took the hill as the Yanks grabbed two from the Bolivar A's: 3-2 in the first and 6-3 in the nightcap.

Bertolini's single in the ninth scored Adam Perlo for the winning run in the opener. Perlo led off the inning with a single and Nidiffer moved him to second with a sacrifice bunt. After a pass ball Perlo scored on Bertolini's hit.

"Bomber" made the lead stand as he struck out one pitching a perfect ninth.

Webster got on the board in the third when Stuckless hit a two-out triple to score Nidiffer from first.

The Yankees regained the lead in the eighth. Santos worked a two-out walk, and McIntyre followed with an RBI double.

Bolivar responded scoring a run of their own in the eighth. Alex Rehnstrom rapped an RBI single to score Ben Titus with the tying run.

Offerman struck out four and walked one in five and a third innings pitched. Gardner struck out two of the five batters he faced.

In the night cap, Johnson got his first start of the season, and the young right-hander who led the team with three yard jobs made it memorable. Johnson struck out three and walked one over six innings of work to get the win. He allowed three runs of which only one was earned. Gardner struck out two in the seventh to get the save.

Webster wasted little time getting after A's starter, Josh Livingston. McIntyre reached base to lead off the second when he was hit by a Livingston pitch. After a Sullivan sacrifice, McIntyre moved up to second and scored on Nidiffer's single. Bertolini kept the inning going with a two-out hit, and Bailey brought both home with a single.

Helmick led the third with a triple and scored on McIntyre's sacrifice fly.

Webster scored two more in the fifth. McIntyre and Sullivan led off with back-to-back singles. After a throwing error advanced the runners, Perlo's ground ball scored McIntyre. Nidiffer followed with his second RBI single of the game.

With the sweep, Webster improved to 11- 15 on the season and moved within two games of a playoff spot.

To continue their streak Webster needed to exorcise any leftover demons from the debacle at Hornell.

Carmody got the ball and scattered six hits over seven innings as Webster downed Hornell 3-1. The left-hander struck out two and walked two to earn his first win of the season.

"Bomber" continued to show his versatility working the eighth and ninth to earn the save. He faced seven batters and was aided by a double play, one of three turned by the Webster infield, to end the eighth.

Stuckless led off the game with his first of three singles on the night. Helmick followed with a run-scoring triple. Santos plated Helmick with a sacrifice fly, and Carmody had all the runs he needed before he took the mound.

Webster added an insurance run in the sixth when Sullivan ripped a two-out single scoring Stuckless from third. Sullivan's hit came after Hornell starter, Matt Davis, issued an intentional walk to McIntyre - whose hitting streak ended at eighteen games. The last time he went without a hit was June 15th. McIntyre entered the game batting .436.

Carmody only allowed one runner to reach second through the sixth inning. The outing was especially satisfying for the lefty who had endured two tough losses. On July first, Carmody limited first-place Allegany County to two earned runs through seven innings but took the loss. He also held Geneva to two runs through seven on June 26th. Again he was saddled with the loss.

Webster improved to twelve wins and fifteen losses. When play opened the following day, two games stood between five teams. Rain prolonged the suspense. Two days later, Webster hosted Elmira.

Elmira entered the game with a league-leading team batting average of .288, and the Pioneers showed why as they banged out seven hits and four runs in the first two innings.

From there, Veenema settled into a brilliant pitching performance limiting the Pio's to two singles over five innings. Elmira did not get a base runner beyond first after the second inning.

"Those first two innings were rough," said Veenema. "I was getting everything up in the zone."

The rough start prompted a visit to the mound from Kelly. "He was honest in his assessment," commented the coach. "He knew they were hitting all of his pitches, but he obviously made the necessary adjustments."

Veenema earned his fifth win of the season. "I got away with a couple in the third, but after that I got my legs under me and started picking my spots."

Kelly went to his bullpen in the eighth, and they didn't disappoint.

Bernath retired the heart of the Elmira lineup in order. Wade Gaynor, Philip Cahill and Jake Wells managed three routine ground balls in the frame. Gardner came on and slammed the door shut in the ninth for his fifth save of the season striking out J.J. Edwards and Mark Carlson before inducing a ground ball from David Valesente.

Bertolini led a thirteen-hit attack with a double, triple, two runs batted in and a run scored. Bertolini's two-out triple in the third gave the Yanks the lead for good.

McIntyre lined a one-out single in the stanza, and Johnson followed with a walk. One out later, Nidiffer added his first of three hits on the evening. McIntyre scored on the hit. Bertolini kept the merry-go-round moving as Johnson and Nidiffer scored. With two hits, McIntyre improved his average to .426 and a league-leading 46 hits and 24 RBI.

Geneva cooled off Webster the next night.

A controversial two-out bases loaded triple in the second proved the difference as the Red Wings trimmed the Yanks 4-3. The play was another in a long list of unfortunate happenings for Kelly's crew. The two-strike line drive appeared to bounce in foul territory, but the shadows created by the night lights clouded the vision of the home plate umpire just enough for the call.

Down 4-0 in the seventh, Webster made a go of it. Helmick rapped the first of four base hits. Santos, McIntyre and Sullivan followed. When the dust settled it was 4-3. So close, but it was not enough.

Bellamy came on and slammed the door in the ninth.

Webster avoided a blowout in the fifth when Geneva loaded the bases. Nick Spears slapped a sinking line drive into center. Stuckless came out of nowhere, made the diving catch, quickly gathered himself and threw to Helmick covering second. Helmick spun and fired to Santos for the unconventional triple play.

Webster dropped to 13-16.

Undaunted, Webster forged on with the season. The following afternoon was Senator Mike Nozzolio day as Brockport visited. The Senator was a strong advocate for the Yanks and the NYCBL working to help assure the existence of the league.

Webster did not disappoint.

Kelly seemed to be finding a winning recipe: strong starting pitching, solid defense, timely hitting, aggressive base-running and a strong bullpen.

DiNuzzo earned his second win of the season striking out three, walking one while limiting the "Bats" to seven hits and two runs over seven innings as Webster won 4-2.

Bernath added relief in the eighth. The native of Stryker, Ohio used a quick move to pick off fellow Toledo Rocket teammate, Aaron Dudley at first. Bernath pitched three innings for the week and limited opponents to one run. Gardner worked the ninth for his seventh save of the season. He now had 33 strike outs in twenty innings of work.

When the pitching needed support the Webster gloves were waiting in a pinch. With two outs and a runner on second Bailey made a diving catch in foul territory down the left field line to retire the "Bats" in the first. Seven innings later Bailey tamed the swirling winds and chased Eric Ferguson's drive to the wall in left-center.

In the fifth, with runners on first and second, the Webster infield turned an inning-ending double play. Helmick snared a Ferguson line drive, tossed to Bertolini who finished the play to McIntyre. Helmick added nine assists on the afternoon.

Bertolini's two-out single, through a drawn infield, scored McIntyre and Sullivan to give the Yanks a 4-2 lead after six.

The Webster offense struck early. Stuckless led the first with a walk. Helmick singled and advanced to second when the speedy Stuckless beat the throw to third. Santos plated both with his first of two base raps on the afternoon.

Stuckless finished the game two for three with a walk.

"I'm happy with the way we're playing," commented Kelly. "We're doing the little things right."

Both Brockport runs came in the fourth. Ferguson led off with a single. One out later, Chad King was hit by a DiNuzzo pitch. The runners moved up on a hit and run play before Jeff Abrams delivered with a single.

Brockport was without Jacob Kaase who earlier in the week signed a minor-league contract with the Texas Rangers.

Webster moved into a tie for sixth place in the NYCBL West with Brockport. Both teams stood at 14-16 and trailed the fourth-place playoff spot by two games. The post-season hung just out of reach.

With just two weeks remaining Brust cautioned: "This is the time of year when it's easy to lose focus. We got things going; we need to keep it that way."

Little did the veteran of many summers know it at the time, but twenty-four hours later he added prophet to his already impressive resume.

Webster traveled to Niagara the following night and, confronted with a case of the "MIA Blues," Kelly cobbled together a lineup that included three pitchers in the batting order. The Webster "Skeleton Crew" came within a base hit in the seventh of tying a game that the Niagara Power eventually won by the score of 5-3.

Curynski attended a family funeral out-of-town. Lawler had a family commitment. Their absences were planned. The other five no-shows caused a problem.

DiNuzzo's two-out double in the second scored Johnson and staked Webster to a 2-1 lead. In his first at-bat of the season Bobby D. sent a one-strike curve ball off the Capitol Cleaners sign in left-centerfield.

Johnson led the frame with a double. The right-hander battled for five innings in his second start of the season. He worked through a bases-loaded jam in the fifth getting Clayton Snodgrass to pop out. Johnson struck out one and allowed eight hits over five innings of work.

Coleman had another strong outing. Two days after getting three outs with his first pitch of a game, Coleman surrendered one run and struck out four over three innings.

Santos and McIntyre continued to work their "A&T magic." With two outs in the first Santos beat out an infield hit. Two pitches later he stole second and scored when McIntyre took a 0-2 pitch the opposite way.

Niagara did most of their damage in the fourth. Trent Thompson lashed a two-out double to score Landis Wilson and Ryan Jacobi. Thompson advanced home on the play because of an error. Niagara added an insurance run in the eighth when Wilson scored on Jacobi's RBI single.

Webster's third run came in the sixth. Bertolini singled and moved up to second when a pick-off attempt sailed into right field. After a balk pushed Bertolini to third, Sullivan walked. When Sullivan's steal drew a throw to second, Bertolini scored.

Gardner just missed tying the score in the seventh. Webster's closer blasted a frozen rope off the 375 sign in left-center field. He was left stranded at second.

Webster dropped to 14-17 on the season with eleven games remaining.

One night later, Geneva again stymied progress. For the second time in four days and third time of the campaign Webster lost to Geneva by a run - this time by the count of 2-1.

Ashton Mowdy scattered five hits over seven innings to lead the Wings. The Mustang, Oklahoma native struck out five and limited the Yanks to one run for his second consecutive win over the Yanks. On June 26th he took a no-hitter into the seventh against Webster before giving up a hit and handing the game to his bullpen.

Andrew Damewood drove in the winning run with a two-out single in the eighth scoring teammate, Chris Vargo. Damewood collected two hits on the night with a run scored.

Julio Gomez ripped a two-out double in the first to score Damewood – the same Gomez who on June 21st hit a two-out three run jack to lead Geneva to a 6-5 come-from-behind victory over Webster.

Kyle Bellamy retired the side in the ninth to pick up the save. The right-hander from the University of Miami eventually finished the season leading the league with 11 saves.

Offerman hurled eight strong for Webster. The big right-hander walked none and struck out five but took the loss. Between the second and fifth innings Gino retired ten consecutive Wing batters. Through seven innings Offerman tossed eighty-eight pitches, sixty-six of which were strikes.

Gardner worked the ninth striking out the side for 36 Ks in 22 innings of work.

Helmick scored the lone Yankee run in the first. After working a walk in a nine-pitch at bat, Helmick advanced to third on a perfectly executed hit and run play. Santos ripped a single into the area vacated by Wing second baseman, Chris Parkinson. Helmick eventually scored on a wild pitch.

Webster squandered their opportunities. In the second and eighth innings, the Yanks led off with back-to-back hits. The inability to execute a bunt and an inning-ending double play cost the Yankees valuable runs. In the seventh, Nidiffer was hit by a pitch, and Adam Perlo followed with a one-out single. Again an inning-ending double play ended the threat.

With the loss Webster dropped to 14-18. More importantly, the Yanks now trailed Geneva by three and a half for the fourth and final playoff spot in the NYCBL West.

Any chance Webster was packing it in for the season was dismissed the following day when the Yanks crushed first-place Allegany County 9-1.

Carmody pitched eight strong, and Santos led an eleven-hit attack.

Carmody set down sixteen consecutive Nitro batters between the second and seventh innings. The lefty struck out eight, walked one and held Allegany County to four hits as he won his second decision in a row.

Webster wasted little time plating runs. Bailey and Santos hit back-to-back one-out singles in the first. Nidiffer's infield single brought home Bailey.

In the second, Johnson took a pitch between the shoulder blades, and Stifler followed with a single. Bertolini dropped a sacrifice bunt. Helmick singled, and the good guys led 3-1. After Helmick swiped his tenth base of the season, Santos delivered him with a double off the fence in left center field. Carmody had more than enough runs.

Nidiffer bid a fond adieu to Nitro starter, Doug Ciallela when he drilled a 1-0 fast ball over the 400ft. sign in deep center to give the Yanks a four run lead.

Chasing Ciallela was particularly satisfying for Webster. It was Ciallela who beat the Yanks on two occasions earlier in the season. On June sixteenth, the right-hander pitched a complete game shutout. For an encore, the Clifton, New Jersey native held the Yanks to three runs over seven and a third for the win on July first.

Webster added two more runs in the fifth. Santos led with a walk, stole second and scored on McIntyre's single. One out later, Lawler singled to left. With runners on the corners, Johnson followed with an RBI sac fly to deep right, and the Yanks took a commanding six-run lead.

The Yanks added two more in the eighth. With two outs Helmick singled and Santos walked. McIntyre bounced a one-hop double off the fence in right center.

Bernath worked the ninth, striking out one of the four batters he faced.

Webster was running out of time.

NYCBL Standings
As of July 19, 2007

Eastern	W	L	Pct.	GB
Glens Falls	25	5	.833	-
Saratoga	19	11	.633	6.0
Watertown	13	17	.433	12.0
Amsterdam	13	19	.403	13.0
Little Falls	11	18	.379	13.5
Bennington	10	21	.323	15.5

Western	W	L	Pct.	GB
Allegany Cty	23	11	.676	-
Elmira	22	13	.629	2.5
Geneva	19	15	.559	4.0
Hornell	19	16	.543	4.5
Brockport	16	18	.471	7.0
Niagara	16	18	.471	7.0
Webster	15	18	.455	7.5
Bolivar	7	28	.200	16.5

Chapter 8

Hanging 'Round the Cage

June melted into July. Spring gave way to summer. The Webster Yankees settled into routines and created a gentle rhythm to the season. Anyone questioning Gino's character need only watch as he orchestrated the crew at home games which filled water coolers and set up tables for concessions. Kelly served as DJ – at least he provided the music at home games. Whether he found salvation in Bruce Springsteen's "18 Tracks," or only had one disc in his vehicle, no one will know. Brust's analytical side provided structure and cohesion to the defense. From game to game, the ex-pro aligned the middle infield with his detailed "spray charts." He noted each opposing at-bat using a combination of dashed, solid and looped lines. The 4" x 5" cards, which hung from a three-ring binder hook in his hip pocket, become a staple of the dugout.

If a rain delay occurred, Brown gladly filled the role as activity director. Fungo golf served as a means to bide time while waiting out thunder and lightning delays. Gardner's bullpen routine divided the team. There were those who saw the reliever as an inspiration. His work ethic served as a model to follow. Others saw Gardner's efforts as intimidating. They had come for a vacation, not to be reminded what it took to become a ballplayer.

No routine was more obvious than that of batting practice. Prior to most games, hitters shuffled in and out of the batting cage taking six swings per turn. Brust presided over this activity. To the casual observer, this custom might appear like nothing more than a leisure activity. To the players, it is much more.

Day after day, night after night, they work on that most identifiable aspect of the hitter: the swing. Fans may focus on whether a player wears his hat with a flat brim as opposed to curled, or if he wears stirrups high as opposed to extending uniform pants to his cleat tops. Players evaluated each other by the swing.

Patience and speed, balance and motion, power and finesse all uncoiled at just the right instant. Hitters use a cylindrically shaped instrument to strike a round object propelled at speeds up to 90 mph - combine this with the prospect of a pitcher using varied grips to create spin and movement, and the task can be daunting. Many contend that striking a baseball is the most difficult task in all of sports. The challenge increases for college players during the summer.

While at school, hitters use aluminum bats. The Northeast-10 (NE-10) is the only remaining conference in the United States which uses wood bats during the season - all other conferences, D1 to junior college, use aluminum bats. Colleges switched to aluminum bats in the early 1970s. The original reason was simple – economics. Wood bats break. Replacing broken bats strains a budget. Since then aluminum bat prices have increased, yet the NCAA stays with their original thinking. The decision creates bad habits.

As Brust explains, aluminum bats with "lighter material and a larger sweet spot create an increased hitting area on the bat. That said; bat speed increases through improper mechanics. Hitters with aluminum bats develop long swings that work for good athletes against the inexperienced pitching they will face in high school, DIII, or less than average DII and DI pitching. Wood bats bring out the truth."

Brust spent the summer helping hitters understand this truth. "I don't have all the answers, but I have some of them." At the same time, the former professional player knew the ground rules. These kids played in the NYCBL for two months. He worked to find those who wanted to learn and spent his time and energy with them.

With Kelly delivering batting practice pitches on the platform halfway between home plate and the pitcher's mound, Brust stood off to the side of the cage sharing his gospel. By late July, one could separate the team into two distinct categories: disciples and apostles.

Disciples came and heard words. They took part in batting practice. From time to time disciples might make eye contact with Brust. An occasional nod of the head indicated the words passed into eardrums. The gesture might have also suggested the youngster had heard enough. Brust knew unsolicited advice found only deaf ears. He figured out for himself during games who simply heard words.

Apostles engaged Brust in discussion. They asked questions often requiring the coach to repeat his answers to confirm they had it correct. McIntyre, Santos, Bailey, Sullivan, "KB", Bertolini and Perlo shared the gospel. Even Gino sought out Brust for a suggestion on switching his grip on the ball. Like an old baseball glove, Brust fit naturally into the role as hitting instructor. He brought with him the days of his youth in Spencerport, New York to the fields of the Advanced-A Carolina League. Those experiences gave Brust a singular understanding of hitting and a hard knocks degree in psychology.

He grew up the youngest of three boys in the farming community just west of the city lines. With its close proximity to downtown, Spencerport offered a varied experience. It was easy for the family to travel to 500 Norton Street and take in a Red Wings game, Rochester's AAA team in the International League. At the same time, the neighboring suburb of Greece provided shopping malls for Brust to connect with friends during his teenage years.

Brust was drawn to the open spaces of Spencerport. Coincidence played no part in this. It was the hand of God that set Brust down on Southridge Drive. Along with his older brothers, Tom and Dan, he grew up in a neighborhood where competition ruled the day. Friends, Mike Valente and Terry O'Grady also strived for athletic gains early in life. Long before the proliferation of youth leagues and camps began offering an endless barrage of numbing structure, the group fashioned its own games and developed a standard of excellence. Needing not the influence of adult supervision, the boys were drawn to the athletic field and in particular baseball.

Brust's older brother, Dan, eventually played college baseball at Brockport State. Valente played under the legendary George Valesente at Ithaca College and helped the Bombers win the 1987 D3 national title. After playing at the University of Buffalo, O'Grady went on to become a pilot in the United States Navy.

As the youngest of the group, Brust quickly learned how to survive. He had no choice. Either he competed or was left out. Those days on Southridge created a focus and tenacity in the young athlete. His drive to excel developed an edge to his game which prepared him for high school sports. When the time came for his decision, Brust did the only logical thing - he enrolled at Cardinal Mooney High School.

Run by the Brothers of the Holy Cross, the Catholic co-ed school was located in neighboring suburb of Greece. The school's location provided convenience.

Its academic standard was outstanding. Its reputation for discipline, spoke for itself. But more than all of those factors, Ed Nietopski coached the Cardinals baseball team.

A product of the St. Louis Cardinals' system, Nietopski came to Rochester in 1953. In his sixth of nine professional seasons, Nietopski roamed the diamond of Silver Stadium at 500 Norton Street along with the likes of Russ Derry and Steve Bilko. He played 96 games that summer, including 87 at shortstop. He continued for three more seasons of professional baseball before returning to Rochester to settle down and raise a family.

Originally, he taught and coached at Brockport High School. When Mooney opened in the 60s, Nietopski made the move. He coached more than two decades on Maiden Lane before the school closed. He finished his career at Bishop Kearney. Upon retiring after 47 years of teaching and coaching, the dean of Rochester high school coaches amassed 545 wins in basketball and 702 victories in baseball – both tops in Section V history.

Brust took his will to win with him to Mooney. He experienced success early. As a sophomore, he earned a spot on the basketball team. In the spring, he was the starting shortstop on the baseball team. A year later, Brust led Mooney to the sectional finals in baseball while earning his second All Greater-Rochester honors. Little did Brust know at the time, he had reached the pinnacle of his high school sports career that season. He spent his remaining time in high school bouncing between the flattery of adoring classmates, the venom of detractors and the criticism of those older than him.

Brust's success on the athletic fields made him well-known in the halls. Many wanted to be Brust's friend and offered praise and adulation for membership in his circle. Others wanted to bring him down to their level. Meanwhile, adults recognized his potential and attempted to keep the young athlete grounded. At the same time, Brust waded through the normal high school experiences of girls, locker room talks and parties.

By his senior season, Brust personified contradiction. On the outside, he wore the physique of a can't-miss athlete. Inside, Brust was a china doll ready to shatter at any moment. Because of his status, classmates looked up to him. Teachers, coaches and family tried to keep him focused. To whom was he to listen? The classmates who praised him? It was nice hearing those words. Or, were his detractors right? Maybe he wasn't that good. Adults offered advice, but like any teenager, it was hard to see it as encouragement.

Brust walked arm in arm with confusion. He viewed the baseball diamond as his sanctuary and despite everything that was happening in his life, his instincts for the game never left him. As his former teammate, Jim Stuver, recalled, Brust did things that no one could teach.

"We were in a sectional game," said Stuver. "The other team had a runner on first with one out when they put on the hit and run. The batter hit a ground ball. The runner took off on contact with his head down. When the runner looked up, Brusty acted like it was pop up. The runner hesitated and looked for the ball. It gave Brusty just enough time to field the ball and complete the double play. He made plays like that all the time - little things that don't get recorded in the scorebook. Don't forget. He was in high school at the time."

Brust graduated from Mooney and left for the University of Maryland. The stakes increased at the Atlantic Coast Conference school. The Terrapins wanted immediate results. Brust showed flashes of brilliance his freshman year, but he never provided what Maryland needed. The pressures and demands of D1 baseball exposed his emotional baggage. Maryland needed a quick fix to their problems. Brust, like any freshman, fell short of fulfilling those needs. He left campus hitting .242 with 17 RBI. Without a mentor, Brust departed College Park and never returned.

He arrived home needing to repair his psyche. Just a year earlier, so much seemed possible. Now, he battled doubt. He needed time to find himself, to find the hope he once had.

Brust quickly took a job bussing tables at a nearby restaurant. The job offered a two-fold advantage. He rose before dawn and started work by six a.m. He finished his shift by two in the afternoon. He was out early enough to play baseball and made enough money to buy the necessary practice equipment.

Once he saved the money, Brust purchased a batting cage which he set up in the back yard at Southridge Drive. The net was 12' high and 20' x 50'. Inside the cage, he hit baseballs from a tee. The curtain had an entry and exit hole where someone could flip him soft tosses with tennis balls. His summer reading list consisted of Charley Lau's The Art of Hitting .300 and The Science of Hitting by Ted Williams. Brust did not just put in time. He reconnected with his earlier success.

He spent the month of May preparing for the summer season with the Cohocton Red Wings of the then Northeast Baseball League. Errant tennis balls dented storm doors. Town sound ordinances were violated. "I didn't want to be singles hitter," said Brust. "When you're desperate to be good, you try a lot of things. I tortured the neighbors."

In high school, he was a "punch and judy" hitter. - a contact hitter, rarely striking out, who was more likely to slap an opposite field single rather than swinging for the fences.

He hung a truck tire from a tree in the back yard with a white spot painted on the treads. Using the largest bat he could find (34), he blasted countless cuts at the rubber. The bat became his weapon as he fought off the second-guessing. With each blast, he released more and more frustration. The sound echoed through the night causing neighbors to call the police. It was all part of the plan: 100 swings in the cage per day and 50-100 hacks at the tire. But that was not the extent of it.

"I was not a fan of the New York Mets, but I loved the toughness of Lenny Dykstra, Keith Hernandez and Darryl Strawberry. I wanted strong hands full of calluses." Brust went through these exercises sans batting gloves.

He found signs of success that summer. He and teammate, Chris Burdick, shared the 70-minute commute along Interstate 390. The duo led the Cohocton Red Wings to the Northeast League title.

That fall he enrolled in classes at MCC.

"Coaches Chamberlain, Bailey, Dawes and Christenson could see my athleticism, but they knew how to help what was under my hat."

Prior to arriving at MCC, Brust played either shortstop or third base. He wanted that to change. He desired more of the action. He wanted to trade in short or third for the position of catcher. He was willing to make the switch from standing to squatting, to exchange fielding grounders for shin guards, a mask and foul tips off the forearms all because he wanted to learn more of the game.

He made the request. Coach Chamberlain listened like any good coach. The two struck a deal. Brust got some time behind the plate (one game), but his bat never left the lineup. He hit .423 with 11 home runs and 49 RBI to earn third team All-American honors. His confidence returned.

"No one could beat me worse than I could beat up myself. They (MCC coaches) told me to just do what they asked, and I would be successful. They helped me re-align priorities." The experience helped Brust learn how to trust a coach. The MCC staff taught Brust about relationships.

He graduated to the Great Lakes Summer League where he played the next two seasons. The second summer he earned an all-star nomination and a trip to Chicago's Wrigley Field for a showcase game. Among others in the lineup for that all-star game was former Cleveland Indian manager, Eric Wedge.

He took the lessons with him as he moved on to Ball State University. There on the Muncie, Indiana campus the transformation manifested. Two weeks after meeting his teammates, Brust was voted captain. His inner drive was infectious. The new teammates recognized him as a winner. He did not disappoint, finishing the season as the Cardinals Most Valuable

Player - this despite some nagging injuries and his first brush with being pitched around. He started hot. Opposing pitchers avoided him. Injuries limited his time in the lineup. Nonetheless, his presence inspired the Cardinals. He followed with a stellar senior campaign. Once again, teammates voted him their captain. He responded with another team MVP and first-team all Mid-American Conference hitting .342 with 14 round trippers.

Possibilities seemed endless.

Brust signed with the Atlanta Braves and spent the summer of 1989 in the Gulf Coast rookie league. In 51 games, he made 186 plate appearances compiling 48 hits, including 12 doubles, three triples and four home runs for an average of .258. He earned another season in the Braves' system and a promotion to the Class A-Advanced League with the Durham Bulls.

The Braves finished that season sixth in the six-team National League West division. For the fifth time in as many years, Atlanta ended the season in one of the bottom two spots of the N.L. West. They fell to sixth the following year. Few knew the Braves were about to reverse their fortunes and become a model of excellence.

In 1991, the Braves claimed the top spot in National League West Division. It was the first of 14 such finishes in the next 15 years. Atlanta's farm system earned the reputation as the best in Major League

Baseball. For three years, Brust played alongside the likes of Javy Lopez, Ryan Klesko and Pedro Borbon - guys who contributed at the Major League level. The Braves stocked their farm system full of prospects. One of the men responsible for evaluating and nurturing the young talent was Grady Little.

Had Brust not known the trust shown him by the MCC staff, he might not have fully appreciated Little. The Durham coach showed Brust professionalism. Little taught the youngsters just as much about life as he did baseball. He showed Brust that mutual respect was something a person should come to expect.

But Brust's chances for advancement were limited. Timing proved itself as an adversary. Things might have been different had he found his way into any other farm system. After two seasons in Durham, he compiled 96 hits including 18 home runs and a bum shoulder. He loaded his belongings and returned to Rochester- his career derailed. He fell short of his dream, but the experience taught Brust how fine of a line existed between a minor league and major league career. He learned how much was possible, and how valuable the investment. Few can give a more accurate measurement for the margin of error between making it and not making it into the big leagues.

Upon his return, he put his equipment away in storage. Save for the occasional jaunt with adult recreation leagues, Brust moved on to other endeavors.

He took classes at Brockport State and earned a Master's in Education before taking a position teaching middle school math at Spencerport. In the spring of 2000, Coach Dawes approached Brust about working the catchers' camp at MCC. Brust agreed. He worked the camp the next five years during which time he met Kelly. Brust became an assistant in MCC during the 2005 season. That summer, he served as Kelly's assistant with Genesee Valley. He followed the younger coach to the Royals the next season before donning pinstripes in 2007.

Almost immediately, Marcus Nidiffer caught Brust's eye. At 6'2" and 180 pounds, the freshman possessed the makings of a ball player – a lean build with plenty of room to grow. Brust recognized the athlete in Nidiffer and saw that the youngster lacked confidence.

He hailed from Bristol, Tennessee and played at the University of Kentucky. Brust used the latter for his nickname: "KB" – short for Kentucky blue. The moniker brought a grin to the youngster's face and the nickname was born.

It didn't take a specialist to figure out what was ailing "KB." The youngster suffered from a lack of at-bats. His first season in the SEC, he earned a grand total of six trips to the plate. On four occasions, he struck out. All he took away from his freshman season was a date with serendipity when he found his way on to ESPN's Sports Center. There was "KB" in the crouch at the receiving end while Roger Clemens worked out with the Wildcats.

His hitting woes continued in the NYCBL. He opened the season 0-1 against Brockport with a walk and a strike out. The walk could have been viewed as a positive except that it seemed as if "KB" did not know when to swing. Undecided, he left the bat on his shoulder and was given a free pass.

Brust took to eradicating any indecision in the young hitter. The solution seemed simple – shorten the swing. He used patience and geometry. "KB" accepted that he needed to shorten his swing. But how would he generate power? There was the trick. Brust showed the youngster to use the angle of the bat and cut the pitcher in half at the waist thus creating more top spin allowing the ball to carry further. Brust gave "KB" a simple exercise – 100 dry cuts a night facing a mirror. Nidiffer followed the regimen – carefully watching the bat angle to assure a shorter swing for attacking the ball.

At first, progress came slowly. Eventually, "KB" created an optimal bat speed. He started squaring up the head of the bat on the ball. Then, it happened. Long, lazy, fly balls turned into line drives. Line drives started finding holes in the defense. "KB" finished the season striking out 28 times – most in the first half of the season. He found the truth in the last ten games of the season driving three home runs, four doubles and a triple.

Bertolini, on the other hand, attacked hitting like he attacked a ground ball. He used everything possible. If he could, Bertolini would dive at the pitch if that created a hit. The "Maytag Man" jumped at the ball. Brust showed him how to let the ball get deeper into the strike zone. As result, Bertolini learned how to drive the ball the other way. When his father, Emil, visited from Ohio, the two could be seen after games in the batting cage behind outfield fence - dad providing the soft toss while the son put into practice Brust's advice.

McIntyre was vastly different from "KB" and Bertolini. He had experienced success in the batter's box. That spring, he led the North Carolina A&T Aggies with sixty-five RBI. He finished second on the team with a .342 batting average and earned his second All-MEAC Team selection. In 2006, he earned MEAC Tournament MVP. He came to Webster wanting to lose weight. At the same time, the left-handed hitter wanted to maintain his numbers. The Carolina native shed more than 30 pounds during the months of June and July. Brust worked with McIntyre on his plate discipline. He needed to take more pitches. As the season wore on, McIntyre became frustrated as opposing teams pitched around him. His 16 walks ranked second on the team and showed his willingness to get better. The two also worked to develop McIntyre's foot speed, so he could play in the field.

Bailey, Perlo, Santos and Sullivan all came through the MCC program. Brust worked with the quartet in the past and wanted to pick up where they left off . Santos and Sullivan needed reminding of lessons past. The two graduated from the junior college and moved to four-year schools. Perlo and Bailey needed to continue what had been started in the spring.

Santos found himself the victim of too many breaking balls. He needed to go back before going forward. Santos hit .379 with 12 HR and 79 RBI for the 2006 MCC team. He needed to find that swing. Brust helped him to reverse his thinking. Santos thought home runs first. The coach got him to focus on singles and let home runs happen. Nelson stopped trying to hit the bottom half of the ball. He shortened his swing and starting using all parts of the park.

Sullivan needed to turn off his brain and learn how to react. Brust recognized that the utility player spent too much time thinking. Sullivan understood how to use the bat. He simply needed to let it happen.

Perlo started the summer jumping at the ball. He swayed and lost his strongest asset: his legs. Time in the turtle for Perlo was spent focusing on letting the ball come to him.   Bailey needed to trust his hands. He was in a rush to get results. Brust encouraged him to slow down and eventually he would drive the ball. Bailey finished the campaign with six hits in the last three games.

The apostles eventually left behind a season in the NYCBL and returned to their campuses, taking with them morsels of Brust's wisdom. He understood failure better than anyone. This characteristic allowed him to help young men appreciate the possibilities they had at their disposal.

Chapter 9

Never Better

By July twenty-fifth, the Webster playoff bus chugged uphill running on fumes. Six games remained. The pinstripes trailed Hornell by five games for the fourth and final playoff spot. Niagara and Brockport also stood in between the Yanks and the post-season.

Suddenly, the reality of the season pressed in like a weight. It was hard to overlook the string of unfortunate happenings that left Webster on the outside of the playoff race. There was the fence that collapsed in Scio costing Webster three runs on what should have been a Santos home run. Instead, the fly ball became the third out of the inning and an eventual two-run loss. Pullyblank's season, cut short by injury, cost the team at least two games in the win column. There was the blown call at first in the third inning of the second game of the year. An inning line that should have read zero runs on two hits and three left on base turned into eight runs on five hits and an error. Up to this point, Webster lost 13 games by two runs or less. Webster personified the adage: "baseball is a game of inches."

Freak occurrences continued. Moments before the July twentieth game in Elmira, Bertolini took a swig from his sports drink. He left the can opened in the dugout as he waited out a rain delay by playing pepper near the outfield fence. Little did he know, a wasp crept into the open container for a taste of the sugary drink. Bertolini rushed in from the outfield to gulp down the beverage and "shhhyyyyyyiiitt!" The insect pierced his upper lip. One inning later, his fleshy fold ballooned to at least twice its usual size. As only Kelly could, the coach made light of the situation. With his lip extending at an angle, Bertolini earned the name of "Mr. Burns" after the Simpsons' character with a similar oral protrusion. The name stuck for the night and Bertolini's mug was the background on none too few cell phones.

Mid-summer storms rumbled through New York. Humid conditions created large banks of clouds which swirled like ice cream in the sky when Gino took the hill against Hornell. Being a mathematics major, Offerman recognized the situation for what it was. The probability of Webster overcoming the odds was nearly impossible. At the same time, Gino did not allow his background with numbers to stand in the way of playing the game he had learned to love since he was a boy growing up on the Caribbean island of Curacao.

Gino faced the minimum in the first. After surrendering a leadoff single he induced a ground ball for double play. His splitter was working. Brust's "spray charts" increased in value as he shifted the defense. The infield readied themselves for a busy night.

A lazy fly to Stuckless ended the frame. Gino had thrown three first-pitch strikes. The stat was not uncommon for an Offerman outing.

One of the five islands of the Netherland Antilles, Curacao is located forty miles off the coast of Venezuela. Roughly 150,000 live on the tiny island that measures 39 miles in length and 22 miles in width. Sitting outside the hurricane belt, Curacao, despite being less tropical than other Caribbean islands to the north, is nonetheless a popular spot for tourists. Like any other vacation spot inhabitants watched as wealthy foreigners came and went – often left to wonder how they could improve their financial status in life.

When native son Andruw Jones broke into Major League Baseball at the age of twenty, locals thought they found a means to financial security. Jones's emergence created a dizzying effect on the tiny island. Suddenly, baseball was seen as a ticket to a glamorous life. Young boys, free from the pressure of a compulsory age for school, began leaving behind books and turned all their efforts to the pursuit of professional baseball. They left Curacao with a dream of playing in the Majors for a fortune only to find that goal far more difficult than imagined. Some wallowed in the minors. Others migrated to Europe and played in the professional leagues across the pond. Soon, disillusioned youths returned to the island without the millions they dreamed of earning and without an education. The situation came close to reaching epidemic proportions. Young men came home to the island virtually penniless and without any prospects for making a living. Fortunately, Gino was only ten at the time. His young age kept him from falling into the trap that befell other youths of the island.

Still, Gino was not immune to the allure of a possible life as a professional baseball player. He experienced success on the diamond. He was barely 16 when he led a team from Curacao to the Latin American championship and a berth in the Senior Little League World Series. He struck out 12 batters in the qualifying round. His abilities were well known throughout the island, and that is why Hensley Meulens became a part of Gino's life.

Nicknamed "Bam-Bam," Meulens signed as a free agent with the New York Yankees in 1985 and spent parts of seven seasons bouncing between the minors and majors. "Bam-Bam" saw first-hand the possibilities offered by playing professional baseball. He also knew the dangers when a young athlete put too much stock in something so uncertain.

It was with that wisdom that Meulens began the Dutch Antilles Baseball Academy. As the name suggested, baseball gave a focus for the organization, but its mission stretched beyond the chalk lines of baseball diamonds. Meulens served as a conduit for the young athletes of the island and prospective colleges in the United States. As part of his mission, Meulens began working to develop a rapport with the younger players of Curacao. Gino was one of "Bam-Bam's" recruits.

As fate had it, Hensley entered Gino's life at a perfect time. Not long after their relationship had been forged Gino's father passed away. At the age of sixteen Gino needed a male role model in his life. Hensley provided the necessary guidance as Gino faced a series of hurdles.

One question that Gino needed answered was his education. Curacao's school model based itself on the Dutch system of VWO, MAVO and HAVO. Under this structure students attended primary school through the age of twelve. At that point, it was decided by counselors, administrators and parents as to an educational track each individual student followed. Students placed in VWO led an intellectual path. MAVO trained for higher-level technical careers. HAVO sought vocational positions. Gino was placed in the MAVO track. He would gain some mathematical experience but not enough to his liking. To pursue his interest in math, it was decided that Gino could take advantage of a foreign student exchange program which allowed him to attend school in the United States.

With her youngest son leaving the country, Criselva Offerman, a seamstress by trade, sent Gino with this wisdom: "You must know how good you are, and how good the people are around you." Gino held on to that practical advice.

Gino headed for Marblehead, Massachusetts. According to law, he was allowed to attend one year of public education in the United States. He enjoyed his time spent in the suburbs of Boston. After his time was up, he needed to find a private school to attend. Meulens was able to get a placement for Offerman in Bangor, Maine.

Bangor did not go well for Gino. Whether it was trouble adjusting to a slower lifestyle than that in Boston or the emotional baggage created by the loss of his father, Gino returned one year later without much to show for his time.

Still, he had not given up on pursuing mathematics, and he had certainly not lost sight of his dream of playing baseball. Meulens interceded and encouraged Gino to continue working. Gino returned to the States where he earned his GED. Once that was in place, Gino moved on to college. From there Meulens helped Gino land at Baltimore City Community College.

It was about this time that Gino began to recognize baseball as a vehicle giving the possibility of education. He was blessed with talents which opened doors to a lifelong career. On the Maryland campus,

Gino began to adjust. By the end of the season, he faced another struggle. Perhaps throwing a splitter had caught up with him. Gino spent that summer nursing the elbow on his throwing arm. The tendinitis was possibly created from the strain placed on the arm from attempting to throw a pitch meant to drop at the plate and render batters incapable of driving the ball into the outfield.

Gino recovered and pitched the following year. It was then that Kelly saw Offerman while on one of Monroe's annual southern trips. Offerman pitched for the Royals in their first year of existence in the league. Kelly didn't need to think twice before asking Gino to return for 2007.

Armed with an unusual wealth of experience for his age and a considerably different perspective from the American players, Gino approached the game on another level. While most, if not all, of the players succumbed to the social pressures around them Gino's life was more based on instincts. This variation helped Gino appreciate what he had and formed his motivations. When a fellow pitcher was taken from the game during an inning, it was Gino who was the first one out of the dugout offering congratulations on a job well done. Unafraid to offer a helping hand, Gino readily shouldered responsibilities of a bat boy. He willingly shagged foul balls and either returned them to play or into the batting practice bag. He was always there to pull stray batting helmets or bats from the field of play and return them to the on deck circle or rack. On the night when Kelly and the Yankees endured the "MIA Blues" in Niagara, it was Gino who put on a catcher's mask and glove and headed for the bullpen to warm up the "Paint Ball Master."

This humble approach also allowed Gino to remain open to suggestions. While knowing he did not have all the answers, he did possess the ability and skill to adapt to new situations and new routines. When Brust suggested changing the grip on his splitter, Gino was all ears. He paid close attention as Brust grabbed a ball and demonstrated. It might have been understandable if Gino dismissed the advice. After all, Brust was a field player. How could he understand the art of pitching? But Gino knew Brust was a student of the game – that no detail of the game was too small for Brust. Gino listened and changed his grip. In his next outing, he gave up two runs on seven hits over eight innings of work. Unfortunately, Ashton Mowdy held Webster to one run over seven before relenting to the untouchable bullpen of Geneva.

On this night, Gino continued a successful string that started with that Geneva game. Free from the possibility of an emotional letdown created by Webster's bleak playoff chances, Gino pitched from the heart. By the fifth, the sun descended, and its reflection cast a pink hue on the friendly cloud bank hanging over the outfield. Under this cotton candy sky, Gino wielded his way through the Hornell lineup.

Every inning Hornell managed to get a base-runner. It was a fact that Gino learned to accept. Since the tendinitis in his elbow his fast ball had lost a touch of velocity. He relied on control and inducing the ground ball. While it is rare for Gino to walk a batter, nonetheless his control means that he is always around the strike zone, and base hits result.

Like always, he worked deliberately, methodically. Once he received the ball, Gino toed the rubber, looked in for the sign, set and dealt. Gino's pace created a rhythm for his fielders which kept them alert and ready. It was something they came to expect. Gino was the conductor leading the orchestra of gloves. As he set for each pitch, his teammates in unison rocked on the balls of their feet with leather ready.

In the sixth, Gino surrendered a one-out bloop double down the right field – a dying quail that touched just inside the chalk and kicked into foul territory. A wild pitch later and Gino found himself not wanting to give in to the Hornell clean-up batter; he surrendered a walk. Showing signs of laboring Gino threw another pitch in the dirt that sped past Nidiffer behind the plate. The catcher spun and retrieved the ball on the grass past the dish. Sliding to his knees "KB" grabbed the pearl and pivoted his torso to deliver a throw. Gino took off from the mound and in one motion slid, blocked the plate, gloved the throw and tagged the runner for the end of the inning.

The play brought everyone in the dugout to their feet as they rushed the field to congratulate Gino. In the press box above, Roger Smith and Kevin Thompson heaped praise on the artistry of "KB" and Gino.

It was a play based on instincts. There was no hesitation on the part of either defender. Gino showed no concern for personal well-being as he slid to block the plate. If apathy gripped a team seemingly eliminated from their goal, this play showed no semblance. It was none of that. For Gino it was how he learned to play the game – with a respect for the importance of each play without regard for the score or playoff implications.

Gino's line read six innings pitched, ten hits, two earned runs, a walk and a strike out. For the summer, he walked five and struck out fifteen in just under 43 innings of work.

Bernath pitched the seventh and eighth.

Gino made his way to the press box and answered questions during the play-by-play transmitted online. He deflected any of the praise showered on him by Smith and Thompson – opting to mention the merits of his teammates. He pointed to "KB's" ability to call a game from behind the plate, and how Nidiffer matured in that area. There was McIntyre who had yet another multi-hit game going four for five with three RBI leading an 18-hit attack. Of course, there was also the leadership displayed by Bertolini at short.

Gardner struck out two in the ninth.

Webster 9 Hornell 3.

Mathematically, Webster was still alive. Things were never better for Gino. He was playing a game from his childhood, and it was helping him earn an education. With his mother's words still ringing in his ears, he was becoming more and more aware of whom he was.

Chapter 10

Finding His Way Back

Sullivan deftly fielded the ground ball, shuffled his feet, set and fired a strike across the Dugan Yard infield to the awaiting McIntyre for the final out of the game.

Webster 4 Bolivar 3.

There was nothing special about the play. The ball gently bounded through the neatly trimmed grass on the campus at St. John Fisher College and easily settled into Sullivan's glove at third. Kevin Thompson and Roger Smith used the cliché tag, "Sunday hop," to describe Sullivan's stop. Umpire Leon Cyrus gave his casual clenched-fist signal for the out. McIntyre trotted across the infield as the team gathered on the third base side of the pitcher's mound.

There was no significant applause to take note.

On the mound, Kevin Carmody exhaled with such force that he nearly lost his balance. Drenched with the sweat brought on by the humid summer evening he raised his eyes to the heavens in a gesture of thanks, and then his shoulders slumped almost involuntarily as his 5'11", 200 pound frame relaxed.

It was a complete game and a win.

149

In the score book, 5-3 (third base to first base for the out) represented the final play. For Carmody, the 27th out of the game stood for anything but a routine play. The ground ball symbolized his redemption. He had found his way back.

As a youngster, Carmody took for granted outings like the complete game on July 25th 2007. Growing up on Long Island, the southpaw attended Massapequa public schools. Competing at the 1AA level, graduates of the Massapequa baseball program regularly went on to play in college. So when Kevin reached the position of #3 starter as a freshman, he had high hopes for the future.

He never knew of the Massapequa program losing more than five games in a season. Each year, the Long Island high school ranked among those considered as contenders for the state title.

A bout with shoulder tendinitis during his sophomore season seemed like nothing more than a bump in the road. He rehabbed the injury and prepared for his junior season – that all-important year in the recruitment process.

Everything appeared on schedule when the unlikely occurred. During the team's annual Spring break trip Florida the coaching staff and a few of the seniors attended a gentlemen's club. News of this reached home and the school district's administration.

By the time the dust settled, administration dismissed the head coach, his assistant and all but five players.

What started as a possible run to the state title with Carmody anchoring the rotation, ended with members of the junior varsity being promoted to help the school field a team. News of the team's misfortune made national headlines. Kevin pitched the final game of the season – a complete game of seven innings, but took the loss 1-0. For his troubles, Carmody earned a spot on ESPN's Sports Center. He knocked a base hit up the middle. It was a small consolation.

In retrospect, the happening triggered a series of pitfalls in which Carmody managed to hurdle each time.

That summer he earned a spot on the Long Island team which competed in the Empire State Games – an amateur event staged in New York State. The annual Olympic-style competition brought together the best athletes from all parts the state. Kevin worked his way to a #5 spot in the rotation. On the surface, it didn't seem like much of an accomplishment. He waited his turn after the first four in the rotation. If Long Island advanced to the medal round, Kevin would get the start. Long Island did not advance. Very few college scouts sat in the stands as he pitched eight scoreless innings striking out 11 and walking none.

Still, Carmody received some correspondence from colleges - Penn State, Hofstra, Franklin Pierce, St. John's and Florida Southern all made contact with the lefty. In the end, Iona College offered the best deal. When all was said and done, Carmody need only pay for his room and board.

After an uneventful senior season in high school, he headed to New Rochelle eager to start fresh.

He was excited when given his first opportunity to start on March 18th, 2005. His excitement waned a little when he realized his first start came against Fresno State. Ready to impress, the freshman took the ball. He soon found out why the Bulldogs annually compete for in the College World Series. Carmody lasted two innings giving up nine hits and eight runs.

Kevin picked up his first win on May fifth when he walked one and struck out one over seven shutout innings as the Gaels downed Fairleigh-Dickinson 4-0. Iona finished the campaign 11-42, but Kevin felt good about the future. He was eager to build on the experience of the first year in hopes of eventually earning a spot as a weekend starter – one of the top three starters in the rotation.

Then he was dealt another blow. Long-time Iona baseball coach, Al Zoccolillo, retired after 18 seasons at the helm.

Once more, Carmody needed to prove himself. This time, he needed to show his new coach, Pat Carey, that he was worthy of a top spot in the rotation.

He prepared for his sophomore season spending the summer in the Atlantic Collegiate Baseball League. He joined the New York Metro Cadets with the understanding that the focus of the team revolved around player development with wins and losses playing a secondary role. Kevin learned differently. Out of 42 games he started two. It was not what the young lefty had in mind.

He returned to campus anxious to get started.

The struggles continued. Against Old Dominion, he came out of the pen and gave up three runs – one earned. Norfolk State scored two earned runs in the two innings pitched by Carmody. The flood gates opened when Lamar tagged him for seven runs – three earned – in one inning. By season's end Kevin was 0-7 with an ERA of 5.75. Of his five starts, he only lasted beyond the fourth once.

Bad luck dogged him. There was the ground ball sure to induce a double play that was bobbled or lost in the exchange. Double plays cannot be assumed. No error gets assigned, and if the benefitting runner scores, the pitcher's ERA suffers.

Carmody refused to surrender. He knew better. He knew what he was capable of accomplishing. That summer he played in the Long Island Federation. He made eight starts and never surrendered more than three hits in an appearance. His confidence showed signs of returning.

What self-assurance he found was difficult to maintain back on campus. Carmody made 13 appearances that spring – six of which were starts. Monmouth touched him for eight earned in five stanzas. Three weeks later, he held Marist to one earned over five but took the loss as Iona fell 8-0. He pitched into at least the seventh in each of his remaining four starts. Still, he ended the season 0-4. The most frustrating performance came against LeMoyne. The Dolphins eventually advanced to the Regionals of the College World Series before losing to Texas A&M and Ohio State. Carmody shut out LeMoyne for seven innings only to have the Dolphins plate the winning run in the ninth.

Undaunted, he packed his bags and headed to Webster for the summer. Some of the players looked at the summer experience as a vacation of sorts. Without parents looking over their shoulder and free from the responsibility of classes, June and July presented the opportunity for a two-month party.

Carmody planned no party. He brought with him an exercise regimen that allowed for only one day off in seven. He quickly acclimated himself to the lay of the land at Oakmonte Apartments. He found the fitness center and learned when the equipment was most available.

After making an appearance in a game, the next day included a 30-minute run with heavy leg lifting –

squats, lunges, squat jumps and scissor jumps. The following day he focused on abdominals – crunches and work with the medicine ball. He worked in a 15-20 minute long-toss session. Days after that included mile runs and a variety of upper body work.

The summer started slowly. He came out of the pen against Niagara and gave up two runs in two innings of work. Four days later, he started, went five and gave up three earned in his first loss of the campaign. A week later, Carmody held Bolivar to two earned runs on six hits while fanning seven over seven. Webster won in extra innings. Bernath got credit for the win. He took the loss on June 26th versus Geneva giving up two runs over six full. On July first, two unearned runs proved the difference and added to Carmody's growing list of losses.

Self-doubt started to seep back into his sub-conscious. He retreated to his freshman year to find a win that meant something. If someone recited Emily Dickinson's lines: "Success is counted sweetest by those who ne'er succeed," Carmody could assure the speaker of those words and their validity.

The slump ended on July 10th. He hurled seven frames holding Hornell to one run on six hits in a 3-1 Webster victory. Eight days later he limited Allegany County to one run on four hits over eight innings while fanning eight in a 9-1 trouncing.

Carmody recaptured a little of his swagger.

His performance on July 25th confirmed what he already knew. Carmody's line read: 9IP, 5H, 3R, 2ER, 2BB, 4SO, 30AB, 34BF. This was what he expected of himself. When he was a freshman on a state contender, he expected to have these outings for the remainder of his career.

What the line score did not indicate was the command Carmody possessed for nine innings. The southpaw painted the corners all night. He cleverly switched speeds keeping opposing batters off-balance all night. The four hits for Bolivar were all singles – none were hard hit. One found the gap on a hit and run. Another was a check swing opposite-field-bloop single. When it was over, Carmody retired the last eleven batters he faced.

The road had been long, but Carmody was back. Success at Iona looked possible.

Chapter 11

Playing out the String...Playing the Spoiler

By July twenty-sixth, Webster's playoff hopes teetered on elimination. A Hornell win or a loss by the pinstripes sealed their fate. Webster had three games remaining on the ledger – Allegany County and a "home and home" with Brockport. There was the possibility of a make-up game at Geneva, but Kelly secretly hoped against having to make the trip. No one could blame him. His thinning squad showed signs of losing any remaining competitive edge.

By this time, Veenema was done for the season. After an unfortunate skirmish during the Niagara game a post-game confrontation ensued in the parking lot. It was decided in the best interest of all involved that Veenema hand in his uniform for the season. The young lefty was caught in a difficult spot. After giving up a three-run dinger in the first, he settled down and retired the next eleven batters he faced. Niagara batters looking to disrupt Veenema's rhythm began calling time after he had his sign. With the umpire granting their wishes, it was inevitable that one pitch would slip, and one did hitting a batter between the shoulder blades.

When the batter turned and took a pair of strides toward the mound, Veenema reacted. Time was called. A heated exchange followed. When the dust settled, Veenema was ejected. The batter remained in the game.

Veenema was not the only departure. DiNuzzo had been experiencing discomfort in his elbow. He shut it down for the season. Helmick returned home for personal reasons. Add those exits to the loss of Pullyblank, and Kelly was running out of choices.

Nonetheless, Webster loaded their vehicles and headed south on route 390 for Scio and a date with Allegany County. The Nitros experienced their own problems. They lost the middle of their order when two players returned home for the summer. At the All-Star Break, Allegany County posted a record of 21-3 and a seven and a half-game lead in the NYCBL Western Division. The Nitros went 3-12 after the break and now trailed Elmira by a game.

Webster jumped to a 2-0 lead in the second. McIntyre led with a single. Sullivan dropped a text book bunt, and McIntyre moved up to second. "KB's" grounder to third base caused some confusion. Instead of taking the easy way out, the defender went for McIntyre who slid safely under the tag. After "KB" stole second, Johnson lifted a fly ball to right. McIntyre scored. Stifler made a rare start and singled home "KB."

Allegany County scored three runs in the fourth on three hits and two Webster errors. A walk, stolen base and a single gave Allegany County a 4-2 lead in the fifth.

Stifler led the seventh with a walk. Gardner, starting in center field, followed with a free pass of his own. Bertolini moved up the runners with a bunt. Lawler singled scoring Stifler. Gardner moved to third, but Lawler was thrown out trying to stretch a single to a double. Santos took four out of the strike zone, and Webster seemed on the verge of blowing the game open with the league's leading hitter, McIntyre, coming to the plate.

McIntyre lashed at the first offering as a bolt of lightning fractured the night sky beyond the fence in center field. A frozen rope bounded off the fence in right center. The scene was eerily reminiscent of that from "The Natural" where Robert Redford rounded the bases with banks of lights crashing in the background. So similar were the scenes that one might have easily imagined Redford coming on for a commercial break and advertising for his new line of "Wonder Boy" bats.

Time was called. The field cleared. Skies opened, and a deluge ensued. Umpires cancelled the game at that point. Originally, Webster received a loss. A misinterpretation of the rules suggested that Webster's seventh inning could not become official until Allegany County had their chance.

Considering the string of misfortune, having runs taken away seemed fitting. The ruling later changed, and the game declared a tie. It all proved moot when Hornell topped Bolivar 6-1.

The only good thing about the following night's game was that it was cut short by rain.

Whether out of necessity or forgetfulness, Kelly trotted Offerman to the hill on two days rest. Without batting an eye Gino took the ball and mowed through the Brockport lineup for five innings. Finally, in the sixth he started missing up in the zone, and Brockport took advantage with three hits scoring two runs.

Gino was done for the game and the campaign.

Webster got a run back in the bottom of the frame when Santos singled home Stuckless.

Johnson came on in the seventh and promptly walked the first two batters he faced. After a bunt moved the runners, a pair of singles plated two. Bernath came on to stop the bleeding. Brockport scored two more before Bernath retired the side. In the eighth, Brockport brought home three more.

Between at bats, the clouds unleashed a downpour. The field resembled a swamp more than a diamond.

Goodbyes started from there. DiNuzzo headed south for Stony Point. Johnson departed for Ohio.

Most of those remaining in town attended a house party that night. The early start time for the next day's game only made matters worse. The season came full circle. What started some 51 days ago at Clark V. Whited Baseball Complex was scheduled to come to a close there on SUNY Brockport campus.

The game meant something for Brockport – they were deadlocked with Hornell for the final playoff spot. Webster was loose, maybe too loose.

Pitching through blood shot eyes, Brown took the hill with a 1-0 lead. The lead did not last. Any question that Brown still felt the effects of last night's, or this morning's liquor, was answered when the he fielded a comebacker, tried to throw out a runner at second and air-mailed the toss into center. Brockport scored two in the frame on three hits and an error. The Riverbats tacked on a run in the third and chased Brown in the fourth with three more.

Webster didn't go down without a fight. Trailing 9-2 in the sixth, the pinstripes strung together three one-out hits. Bailey got it going with a base rap. Stuckless followed with a double. Bailey scored on Bertolini's two-bagger. One out later, McIntyre brought the pair home before the side was retired. In the ninth, Webster put another across the plate. McIntyre led with a triple and scored one out later on Stifler's single.

Brockport 9 Webster 6.

Before going their separate ways, Kelly mentioned the possibility of a make-up game the following day. Chances seemed remote.

Remote happened. Geneva shut out Elmira and now led by a half game, requiring another game. For Geneva, the solution was simple: win and take the division title. With a loss the Red Wings dropped into a tie with Pios. Based on head-to-head play, Elmira grabbed first place. Geneva had to like their chances. They were 5-0 versus Webster on the campaign. But four of those victories came by a total of five runs.

Sunday's turnout for Webster was so scant that Gino stepped in and took a few hacks during batting practice. He left the cage mumbling: "I still can't hit the deuce."

Coleman got the start on the mound. The "Paint Ball Master" came into the game limiting opponents to one run over his previous thirteen innings pitched. During that string, he shut out Geneva over four frames.

When Webster took the field in the bottom of the first, Brust gave a measured look around the diamond and voiced his approval of the day's lineup. Those that remained were there to play baseball – score and record mattered little to them. The dugout, which Brust had described earlier in the season as a coffee house with too many different conversations, was quiet. Only Brust, Kelly, Gino and "Bomber" remained on the pine.

Coleman's shutout string quickly became a thing of the past. After a leadoff single, Coleman fielded a sacrifice bunt and sent the throw down the right field line. Gardner, playing right field, alertly scooted down the line and retrieved the ball, but the damage was done. By the time everyone caught their breath, Geneva pasted a deuce on the McDonough Park scoreboard.

Webster refused to give in to the situation. Down 5-1 after three, the pinstripes fought back. Santos singled to right. McIntyre walked. "KB" brought them home with a blast that could not get over the fence in left center quick enough. Webster's dugout bounced with energy.

Two days after tossing six at Scio, "Bomber" took the hill and pitched five scoreless innings.

Webster pulled away in the sixth. Adam Perlo led with a single. Bailey proved he too could swing the shillelagh as he sent a frozen rope over the fence in the left. Gardner walked and stole second. It didn't matter; Stuckless also received a free pass. Both moved up 90' on a passed ball. Gardner was thrown out at home on a fielder's choice. One out later, McIntyre walked, and "KB" brought home a pair when his infield single induced a throwing error. Perlo finished what he started with a pair of RBI. Webster led 11-6.

For the remainder of the game, no one else crossed the dish.

Bailey led the seventh with a double – his third hit of the game. Brust's gospel was paying dividends. Gardner displayed his ability with the bat. With Bailey on second, Gardner fought off several pitches before pushing the ball to the right side of the infield. Bailey moved up to third.

After "Bomber" retired the Red Wings in the seventh, Gardner made a bee line for the bullpen. Gino grabbed a glove and mask and joined him. Gardner was the same player on the last day that he was the first.

He did not need to don the hooded sweat shirt as usual. He was plenty warm from playing the field today. He already had done plenty of sprints, so running along the outfield fence was not necessary. First, it was the stretch bands. Then, the towel used to help him reach for the plate. Quickly, he took out the nine ounce green ball and tossed a few. A few fast balls, a couple curves and then a change or two before going back through the tosses again. He was ready.

Gardner maintained his focus on an objective but never lost sight of the process. He signed with Webster for the expressed purpose of establishing himself as a closer. He set a goal for himself at the beginning of the season to fan 40 batters. Rather than solely focusing on his goal and losing sight of everything around him, he took advantage of all the opportunities provided him. Today, he played in the field for the eighth time on the season. He made a heads-up play down the right field line backing up a throw. He bagged two hits, stole a base and showed his ability to hit behind the runner. When Geneva came to the plate in the ninth, Gardner retired the side in order with one strike out – his 37th of the year.

Geneva settled for second.

After the game, Kelly made arrangements with the remaining players to get their uniforms. "KB" was ready to head back to Tennessee. Gino and McIntyre returned to the Oakmonte Apartments and packed their gear. McIntyre had a train to catch in the morning. Gino was still uncertain about his travel plans.

Kelly loaded up the Element, turned the key and plugged in his I-Pod. Springsteen filled the speakers.

Webster Yankees at Geneva Red Wings
Jul 29, 2007 at Geneva, NY (McDonough Park)

Webster Yankees 11 (18-24)

Player	AB	R	H	RBI	BB	SO	PO	A	LOB
Stuckless cf............	5	1	1	1	1	0	2	0	1
Bertolini ss.............	5	1	1	0	0	0	2	5	4
Santos 3b...............	5	1	2	0	0	2	0	2	0
McIntyre 1b.............	3	2	0	0	2	0	13	1	0
Nidiffer dh.............	4	2	3	4	1	1	0	0	0
Sullivan lf.............	4	0	0	0	1	0	0	0	2
Perlo c.................	5	1	2	2	0	1	5	0	0
Bailey 2b...............	5	3	3	2	0	0	2	3	0
Gardner rf/p............	4	0	2	0	1	0	3	0	0
Coleman p...............	0	0	0	0	0	0	0	1	0
Curynski p/rf..........	0	0	0	0	0	0	0	1	0
Totals..................	40	11	14	9	6	4	27	13	8

Geneva Red Wings 6 (26-16)

Player	AB	R	H	RBI	BB	SO	PO	A	LOB
Hypke 3b................	4	1	1	1	0	0	0	0	3
Miller rf...............	4	2	1	0	0	1	0	0	1
Laplante rf.............	1	0	0	0	0	1	0	0	0
Damewood lf.............	4	0	2	2	1	0	2	0	0
Gomez c.................	4	1	1	0	1	1	4	2	1
Parkinson 2b............	4	1	1	0	1	0	5	3	0
Stokes 1b...............	3	0	1	1	1	1	10	0	1
Vargo cf................	4	1	1	1	0	0	4	0	2
Daleiden dh.............	3	0	0	0	0	1	0	0	0
Summers dh.............	0	0	0	0	1	0	0	0	0
Spisak ss...............	4	0	2	1	0	0	2	4	2
Rhodes p................	0	0	0	0	0	0	1	0	
Purington p............	0	0	0	0	0	0	0	1	0
Forster p..............	0	0	0	0	0	0	0	0	
Schiller p.............	0	0	0	0	0	0	0	0	
Totals..................	35	6	10	6	5	5	27	11	10

Score by Innings	R	H	E
Webster Yankees..... 001 406 000 -	11	14	1
Geneva Red Wings.... 212 100 000 -	6	10	5

E - Coleman(1); Damewood(1); Parkinson(1); Spisak 3(3). DP - Yankees 1; Red
Wings 2. LOB - Yankees 8; Red Wings 10. 2B - Bailey(1); Damewood(1);
Spisak(1). HR - Nidiffer(1); Bailey(1). HBP - Vargo. SF - Hypke(1);
Stokes(1). SB - Santos(1); Gardner(1); Miller(1). CS - Bertolini(1).

166

Webster Yankees	IP	H	R	ER	BB	SO	AB	BF
Coleman.............	3.0	8	6	5	3	1	16	21
Curynski............	5.0	2	0	0	2	3	16	19
Gardner.............	1.0	0	0	0	0	1	3	3

Geneva Red Wings	IP	H	R	ER	BB	SO	AB	BF
Rhodes..............	3.0	3	1	0	0	2	11	11
Purington...........	2.0	6	7	5	3	1	13	16
Forster.............	1.0	3	3	0	3	0	5	8
Schiller............	3.0	2	0	0	0	1	11	11

Win - Curynski (1-2). Loss - Purington (1-4). Save - None.
WP - Curynski(1). HBP - by Coleman (Vargo). BK - Schiller(1). PB - Gomez(1).
Umpires - HP: Warren Bumpus 1B: Carmen Perrioti
Start: 3:00pm Time: 5:30pm Attendance: 212
Coleman faced 2 batters in the 4th.
Purington faced 3 batters in the 6th.
Forster faced 1 batter in the 7th.
Game: GRWY0729

Box score courtesy of www.nycbl.com

167

Afterword

Elmira swept their way to the '07 title. After dispatching Hornell 5-0 and 4-3, the Pios advanced to the finals beating Geneva with a pair of six packs – 6-3 and 6-1. Glens Falls offered little resistance as Matt Burch's crew won 14-4 and 9-5.

Gardner's Ithaca College teammate, Shane Wolf, earned Player-of-the-Year honors. Wolf finished the season hitting .367 with 11 RBI for Elmira. The Freeville, N.Y. native made eight appearances on the bump going 5-1 with an ERA of 1.31.

Gardner earned second-team All-NYCBL honors. In 22 appearances, he tossed 26 frames facing 83 batters surrendering 9 hits (none for extra bases), 13 walks and four earned runs while fanning 37 for an ERA of 1.38.

The Ithaca Bomber teammates both heard their names called in the 2008 MLB draft. Houston chose Wolf in the 26th round. Gardner went to Cincinnati in the 34th.

Wolf played the summer of '08 in the New York-Penn League for the Tri-City Valleycats.

Gardner started his summer with the Gulf Coast Reds. Working primarily as a set up man, the lefty tossed 22 innings in 18 appearances fanning 25, walking 11 while posting an ERA of 4.50. For his efforts, Gardner earned a playoff spot with the Billings Mustangs of the Pioneer League.

Finishing the season with a league-leading 65 hits, 16 doubles, 89 total bases and a batting average of .409, McIntyre grabbed first-team honors. Coupled with his 65 RBI for North Carolina A&T that spring McIntyre earned his way on the Brooks Wallace Award Watch list. The prestigious award is given annually to the nation's best college baseball player. The award honors the memory of former Texas Tech shortstop and coach who died at the age of twenty-seven after a long battle with cancer.

Seven other NYCBL alum dotted the Wallace Watch: Chris Dove (Saratoga '06/ Elon), John Allman (Amsterdam '04/ Kansas), Tim Alberts (Geneva '06/ Niagara), Jake Owens (Glens Falls '07/ Northwestern), Mark Kelly (Glens Falls '07/ Southern Illinois), Sean Barksdale (Allegany County '07/ Temple) and Ollie Linton (Little Falls '06/ UC-Irvine).

2008 did not go as well for McIntyre or for the Aggies. McIntyre and Santos did not get a call the day of the MLB draft.

Mike Kelly accepted the head coaching position at Monroe Community College. In his first season, the former bullpen catcher led the Tribunes to a school-record 41 wins and third place in the NJCAA Division II

World Series. His school responsibilities caused him to leave behind the NYCBL.

Brust gladly seized the reins and ran with it. The new head coach wasted little time reconnecting with old friends. He called Ken Harring, an old teammate from his days with the Durham Bulls. Harring sent three of his players from the University of Massachusetts-Lowell. Brust contacted his former head coach at Ball State, Pat Quinn who now worked in the athletics' office at the university. Three Cardinals planned to make their way to Webster for the summer.

Webster's 2008 version was taking shape.

Gino landed at Indiana University of Pennsylvania. During pre-season, he experienced some tightness in his throwing arm. Before permanent damage occurred, it was decided he would red shirt the season. The misfortune made Gino eligible for another season in the NYCBL, and the native of Curacao planned to summer in Webster until IUP's class schedule changed. Needing to take one course during the summer to stay on track for graduation, Gino stayed in Pennsylvania for the summer. Originally, the class was scheduled to be given online. That changed, and so did Gino's plans.

DiNuzzo went home to a pair of MRIs. The procedure showed a stress fracture in his elbow. His MCL was pulling on the bone and caused the break. Surgery was not needed. DiNuzzo got by sleeping with a bone stimulator on his arm. The rehabilitation was the same for a "Tommy John" surgery.

DiNuzzo and Carmody finished out their careers with a doubleheader loss to LeMoyne. DiNuzzo earned two of Iona's four wins for the season as the Gaels failed to qualify for the conference tournament.

Pullyblank spent the fall semester in Rochester while his arm recovered from surgery. In the spring, he moved on to Southern Illinois University where he teamed up again with Curynski.

"Bomber" struck out 33 and walked 19 in 49 and a third innings of work for the Salukis. He posted a team-best ERA of 2.37 while going 5-1.

Bertolini started 51 games for Mercyhurst hitting .319 with seven doubles, one round tripper and 18 RBI. The "Maytag Man" led the Great Lakes Intercollegiate Athletic Conference in assists while compiling a fielding percentage .964 to earn a spot on the North Central Region Gold Glove team. He played the following summer in the Independent Frontier League with the Midwest Sliders before taking the position as head coach of Mercyhurst North East – a junior college branch campus of his alma mater.

Adam Perlo adjusted to first base at Hofstra. After experiencing considerable success at Monroe, Perlo and Stuckless adjusted to some losing as the Pride went 19-36. Perlo managed 10 hits in 31 at bats including a home run and nine RBI. Stuckless had 27 hits and scored 20 runs.

"KB" split time behind the plate for Kentucky. He made 34 starts for the Wildcats hitting a modest .216, but Nidiffer went deep five times with 17 RBI.

Sullivan and Veenema helped the University of Rochester finish 28-13. Sullivan hit .340 in 28 starts with 35 hits, 25 runs, and 20 RBI. Veenema went 7-2 in 12 appearances with 58 strike outs and 28 walks.

Sullivan, Bailey, Bernath, Curynski and Adam Perlo all signed on to play for Webster in 2008.   The rest of the faces changed, but the season was eerily reminiscent of the year prior.

Bob Shaffer and Dave Parlet joined Brust's staff. They brought with them plenty of experience. Shaffer played at MCC with Mark Perlo before he moved on to pitch at Florida International. Since then, the high school business teacher logged hours with the pitching staffs of community colleges in the Rochester area.

Parlet balanced his time between serving as a scout for the Chicago Cubs and private instruction.

The experience of the staff proved invaluable as the young club faced an endless line of pitfalls.

On the surface the Yanks' posted a record of 17 wins and 24 losses.

Of their 41 games played during the months of June and July, 20 were decided by two runs or less. Ten of those games Webster lost by one run. The difference between being a competitive team and a playoff team was measured by an inch here, an inch there, a play here and a play there.

With a handful of league honors and a host of personal accomplishments, the 2008 Webster Yankees showed themselves as more than worthy adversaries.

Luke Wallace (UMass-Lowell) started the season with a bang. Wallace's two-run home run in the eighth inning proved the difference as the Yankees opened the season with a 6-4 win in the first game of a double-header at Bolivar. Wallace went on to lead the club with three round-trippers – his third served as a bookend for the season coming in the finale at Hornell.

Wallace led five Yankees who went yard on the season.

Drew Hormann planted a shot over the left-center field fence in a Yankee victory over the Niagara Power on June 29th. Hormann fell a single short of the cycle that afternoon.

Hormann's college teammate at Miami of Ohio, Kyle Weldon, slapped a solo shot in a losing effort against Hornell. Weldon finished the season hitting .282 with 12 RBI. The Mason, Ohio native collected four hits in the Yanks victory over Elmira in the first game of a doubleheader on July 6th.

Sullivan went deep twice in a later triumph over the Power. Sully earned NYCBL Player-of-the-Day honors as he went 3-4 with five RBI and three runs scored. He was one of five Yankees to earn the NYCBL honor.

Aaron Etchison (Ball State) nabbed the award early in June when the red-shirt freshman from Pendleton, Indiana slapped a one-out bases loaded double to help the home nine come back from a five-run deficit to defeat eventual NYCBL champ, Brockport. "Etch" finished the campaign with eight doubles and eight RBI.

Curynski tossed a complete-game shutout on June 29th to earn the NYCBL honor. Coupled with eight shutout innings earlier in the week, "Bomber" garnered the Western Division Pitcher-of-the Week. Going 16 innings for the week without allowing a run, he lowered his ERA to 1.34. Curynski finished the summer with 34 strike outs and 21 walks in 54.2 innings of work. "Bomber" tossed one inning in the NYCBL All-Star Game and was credited with the win as the West topped the East 9-5.

John Kenny (Hofstra) also earned dual-league honors. The speedy outfielder went six for nine with a walk-off single as the Yanks swept a double header from the Elmira Pioneers on July sixth. The Franklin Valley,

New York native led the league with 13 hits for the week including one home run and seven RBI for Player-of-the-Week honors. Kenny had four multi-hit games and a pair each of multi-RBI and runs scored contests in the seven-day period. The sophomore led the club with 24 base on balls and 28 runs scored.

Steve Muoio's (Georgia College) team-leading batting average of .375 was good enough for third in the league. The hometown boy also led the Yanks with 48 hits, 20 RBI and 12 extra base hits.

Cory Brownsten (Pittsburgh) and T.J. Baumet (Ball State) led the way with three triples a piece. Brownsten finished the summer with 19 RBI and 19 runs scored. Baumet proved his ability to perform in the clutch collecting nine two-out hits for the season producing nine RBI in those situations.

Matt Zahel (Toledo) finished the season hurling 16 and a third consecutive shutout frames. He posted a team-leading ERA of 1.65 - striking out 26 while walking 12 in 32 frames on the rubber.

Sam Dawes (Miami of Ohio) won three games and saved two for the season. Dawes struck out 35 and walked 14 in 35 innings. The southpaw put opposing hitters in lock down holding them to a miniscule average of .190.

Pat Urckfitz saved two before his NYCBL season was cut short when he signed a contract with the

Houston Astros. In seven appearances for Webster, Urckfitz fanned 25 and walked five in 14.2 innings. The left hander made 15 appearances for the Greenville Astros of the Appalachian League posting an ERA of 1.40 with 23 whiffs and nine walks. With those numbers, Urckfitz earned an invitation to the Astros fall instructional league in Kissimmee, Florida.

Ryan Schreiber (Mercyhurst) and Dom Sapp (MCC) joined the club after the departure of Urckfitz. Schreiber worked 27 innings picking up the win in the second game of the doubleheader sweep of Elmira. Sapp introduced NYCBL hitters to his "ghost" pitch while working 24.2 innings for the season. With his variation of a change up Sapp struck out 27 and finished with a record of 2-1 and an ERA of 2.19.

Versatility belonged to Geoff Dornes (R.I.T). Against Brockport late in the season, Dornes went from the field, to the plate, to the mound in successive innings. After running down a fly ball forty yards away in foul territory, the lefty from Landisville, Pennsylvania drove in the eventual winning run with two outs in the ninth as the Yanks topped Brockport on July 29th. After getting the job done at the plate, Dornes took the hill and closed out the game for his first save of the season. The two-time Empire 8 Conference Player-of-the-Year finished the season with 34 hits and a batting average of .301. He struck out 25 and walked 10 in 43 stanzas on the mound.

Theft became the department of Bailey. The Webster native led the team with eight stolen bases in ten attempts.

Adam Perlo demonstrated a penchant for timeliness. Mired in a slump, the Fairport native busted out with a pair of RBI against Niagara and a rally-hopping single in the Webster comeback victory over Brockport.

The Webster infield turned 27 double plays for the season. Mark Wiggins (UMass-Lowell) had a hand in several of those efforts. The freshman also slapped four doubles and a triple on the season.

Jacob Bernath returned and provided a lesson in fearlessness. After taking a line drive in the jaw, the lefty recovered and finished the season striking out 19 and walking 12 in 30 innings work.

Inspiration came from Dustin Ramey (UMass-Lowell). Less than a year and half removed from "Tommy John" surgery to replace the ulnar collateral ligament in his pitching elbow, Ramey went on to lead the club with four victories. Webster fans watched as Ramey pitched in a game for the first time since the procedure. Starting out on a pitch count and working three innings for his first two appearances of summer, Ramey eventually worked his way up to five innings. In 31.2 stanzas of work Ramey fanned 29 and walked 9.

Anthony Gionesi (Hofstra) learned a lesson in perseverance. The big right hander from North Bellmore, New York worked 47.2 innings on the season (second only to Curynski). He struck out 30 and walked 17, yet for all his efforts came away without a win for the season.

In the final count, the Yankee efforts were best measured against the top teams of the Western Division.

Webster finished the '08 season with a record of four wins and two losses against eventual league champion Brockport. The Riverbats won six of their seven post-season games including two of three against Eastern Division foe, Glens Falls.

The home nine finished one and five against first-place Hornell, but four of those losses were decided by a total of five runs.

2008 wasn't done and plans were being made for '09. Mark Perlo banged on some more doors. This time though, his team had a home field. Ground was broken on Basket Road Field. Maybe he could actually sit back and enjoy the upcoming season.

Brust started building another roster. June wasn't far away and with it would come another season in the New York Collegiate Baseball League. A season filled with hope and possibility.

NYCBL Alumni, 2007 MLB Draft

Rd. Name (School) MLB Team NYCBL Team
5 Zach Lutz (Alvernia) - New York NL - Hornell '07
11 Andrew Groves (Purdue) - Colorado - Amsterdam '05
11 Matt Bouchard (Georgetown) - New York NL - Plattsburgh '05
13 Jordon Wolf (Xavier) - Baltimore - Amsterdam '05
15 Ryan Eigsti (Bradley) - Kansas City - Hornell '05
15 Keith Meyer (Duquesne) - Seattle - Gen. Valley '06
15 Ryan Hill (Rutgers) - San Diego - Glens Falls '04
15 Chris Garcia (St. Petersburg) - Los Angeles AL - Amsterdam '07
15 David Williams (Rutgers) - New York AL - Glens Falls '04-'05
16 Adam Campbell (New Orleans) - Florida - Glens Falls '06
16 Darin Mastroianni (USI) - Toronto - Saratoga '06
17 Brian Espersen (Mercyhurst) - Houston - Hornell '06
17 Levi Maxwell (West Virginia) - Chicago AL - Watertown '05
20 Jose Made (Dominican) - Chicago NL - Bennington '07
22 Jake Rogers (South Dakota St) - Washington - Hornell '06
23 Jacob Kaase (TX Lutheran) - Texas - Brockport '07
24 Jonathan White (Vanderbilt) - Milwaukee - Glens Falls '06 - Did not sign
24 Caleb Mangum (NC State) - Philadelphia - Saratoga '04
24 Jimmy Dougher (Cortland St) - Toronto - Glens Falls '05
24 Michael Parker (George Wash) - New York NL - Amsterdam '04
25 Cliff Flagello (Shorter) - Baltimore - Plattsburgh '05
34 Tom Hill (Albany) - Kansas City - Glens Falls '04
35 Thad Weber (Nebraska) - Cincinnati - Alfred '04 - Did not sign
40 Dallas Cawiezell (Valpo) - Cleveland - Glens Falls '06
41 Jordon Herr (Pittsburgh) - Chicago NL - Rochester '06 - Did not sign
41 Tom Edwards (Rutgers) - Texas - Little Falls '07 - Did not sign
42 Joe DiGeronimo (Wagner) - Baltimore - MV '05/LF '06

Free Agent Signings
Bobby Hastry (Marist) - Kansas City - AM '06/WAT '05
Vinny Pennell (Franklin Pierce) - Kansas City - Watertown '05
Brendan Monaghan (St. John's) - Baltimore - Hornell '05
Chris Rosenbaum (Tampa) - Los Angeles (AL) - Watertown '04, '06

List compiled by John McGraw for nycbl.com.

Acknowledgments

So many people gave freely of their time to help me with this project. Thank you all.

I am grateful for the 2007 Webster Yankees who welcomed me into the clubhouse and made me a part of the team. Here's hoping everyone had half as much fun as me. Any time you guys need somebody to shag flies, just give me a call. There's nothing like running barefoot in the outfield grass. Thanks to those who sacrificed time to sit and answer questions or return my phone calls: Dave Brust, Kevin Carmody, Coach H. David Chamberlain, Bryan Gardner, Mike Kelly, Eugene Offerman, Brian Pullyblank and Mark Perlo. Special thanks to Brusty, Mike, Gino and Mark for reading chapters and providing feedback.

Several friends volunteered to read individual chapters. They did so without any hesitation - this despite the whimsical nature in which I requested help. Thanks to Joe Ditucci, Donna & Paul Hardmeyer, Pete Montenaro, Patrick Reynell, Aaron Smith, Beth Smith and Chris Wuest for taking the time to read, comment and offer words of encouragement.

I am indebted to Christopher Shannon who gave the title to this book. Chris spent numerous hours on the phone reading and editing chapters. Thanks also to my mother-in-law, Margaret McCabe, who took the time to read through each of the chapters. Let the joke begin – Paul asked an 81-year-old woman with one good eye to edit his book.

Deb McGwin wasted no time capturing the spirit on the book cover. I have learned not to judge a book by its cover. Here's hoping this story lives up to the design created by Deb. You can find more of her work at debmcgwinphotoanddesign.com. Ryan Sullivan graciously provided the items for the front cover. I called him and in less than 24 hours, he delivered. Thanks Ryan. Many thanks go to Vince Falbo. He provided guidance for the book's website. I asked and Vince gave answers. It was a joy to collaborate with Courtney Green on the website design. After my daughters, Courtney holds the distinction of playing more games for me than other student-athlete I have coached. Thanks for helping Court!

Thanks to my sister, Beth, for giving up part of her summer to take pictures. Thanks also to her husband, Roger. He tagged along for the ride and, at times, grabbed the wheel. It was Roger who was driving when I got the idea to spin this tale. It was a late night returning from Niagara Falls on the Lake Ontario State Parkway when I realized there was more to this than writing game reports.

Thanks to the leagues of the NACSB – the Atlantic Collegiate Baseball League, Cape Cod, Central Illinois Collegiate, Florida Collegiate Summer, Great Lakes, New York Collegiate Baseball and the Valley Baseball League.

These leagues, with their steadfast commitment to statistics and other items on league websites, provided valuable sources of information which allowed me to gain a deeper understanding of summer wood-bat leagues.

Thanks to Kathy Blasi who provided insights into the world of publishing.

I could not have completed this project without the patience of Jason Bates and the help of everyone at Mercury Print Productions.

None of this would have happened if it was not for the love and support of my wife, Kelly, and our daughters, Abbey and Cece. It was Kel's words: "We should get you a lap top," which set this book in motion. Though I can't be sure, there might have been some prodding from Abbey and Cece. After all, I was taking away their precious time on the family computer. I am blessed to have you in my life. "I'll work for your love any day."

Please support PickinSplinters.com – 'Cause there's always room for one more on the bench. Check out the Chinchillas! The best rock 'n' roll band that not enough people have heard.

"Do unto others as you would have others do unto you."

Player	AVG	GP-GS	AB	R	H	2B	3B	HR	RBI	TB	SLG%	BB	HBP	SO	GDP	OB%	SF	SH
McIntyre...	.409	41-41	159	30	65	16	1	2	36	89	.560	16	4	18	4	.472	1	0
Stuckless...	.326	33-33	129	19	42	6	1	0	9	50	.388	11	1	11	1	.380	1	4
Santos...	.287	41-41	157	28	45	10	0	2	18	61	.389	20	2	40	0	.372	1	0
Stifler...	.273	15-12	44	4	12	2	0	0	7	14	.318	6	0	14	1	.353	0	0
Bailey...	.250	29-27	104	14	26	9	2	1	12	42	.404	4	2	31	3	.291	0	3
Helmick...	.245	29-27	106	20	26	6	1	1	5	37	.349	9	2	12	3	.310	0	2
Sullivan...	.234	31-28	94	10	22	2	1	0	10	26	.277	14	3	11	3	.348	1	3
Nidiffer...	.227	30-28	97	13	22	4	1	3	12	37	.381	11	1	28	0	.339	1	2
Johnson...	.221	33-31	122	14	27	2	0	3	20	38	.311	9	1	28	2	.276	2	0
Bertolini...	.193	37-36	135	15	26	3	1	0	16	31	.230	7	0	14	1	.229	2	7
Lawler...	.188	35-34	133	13	25	4	1	2	11	37	.278	7	0	33	2	.227	1	0
Perlo...	.184	21-20	76	6	14	0	0	0	4	14	.184	2	2	17	1	.225	0	0

DiNuzzo...	.333	1-1	3	0	1	1	0	0	1	2	.667	0	0	1	0	.333	0	0
Gardner...	.240	9-8	25	2	6	1	0	0	0	7	.280	4	0	5	1	.345	0	2
Carmody...	.000	1-0	1	0	0	0	0	0	0	0	.000	0	0	0	0	.000	0	0
Totals...	.258	41-41	1392	189	359	66	9	14	162	485	.348	121	24	266	21	.326	11	23
Opponents...	.265	41-41	1383	211	366	51	9	6	185	453	.328	151	47	262	15	.355	9	28

(All games Sorted by Earned run avg)

Player	ERA	W-L	APP	GS	CG	SHO/CBO	SV	IP	H	R	ER	BB	SO	2B	3B	HR	AB
Gardner.....	1.38	0-1	22	0	0	0/0	4	26.0	9	7	4	13	37	0	0	0	83
Carmody.....	2.70	3-3	8	7	1	0/0	0	50.0	42	20	15	16	31	7	1	2	187
Curynski....	3.12	1-2	10	4	2	0/0	2	40.1	27	19	14	19	38	3	2	1	143
Veenama.....	3.43	4-3	7	7	0	0/0	0	42.0	45	26	16	15	31	5	1	1	166
DiNuzzo.....	3.53	2-4	7	7	0	0/0	0	43.1	44	22	17	10	34	0	0	0	164
Offerman....	4.22	3-4	8	7	0	0/0	0	42.2	61	28	20	5	15	11	2	0	185
Bernath.....	4.26	1-1	20	0	0	0/0	0	31.2	33	19	15	10	15	7	0	0	119
Coleman.....	4.94	0-0	16	1	0	0/0	0	31.0	33	21	17	21	23	2	0	0	115
Brown.......	6.40	1-3	13	4	0	0/0	0	32.1	50	30	23	15	18	8	3	0	134

McIntyre....	0.00	0-0	1	0	0	0/0	0	1.0	0	0	0	1	1	0	0	0	3
Pullyblank..	2.63	0-1	3	3	1	0/0	0	13.2	10	7	4	7	9	3	0	1	49
Johnson.....	12.00	0-1	3	1	0	0/0	0	9.0	12	12	12	7	3	1	0	1	35
Totals......	3.89	15-23	41	41	4	0/0	6	363.0	366	211	157	151	262	51	9	6	1383
Opponents...	3.58	23-16	41	41	4	3/2	8	365.0	359	189	145	121	266	66	9	14	1392

New York Collegiate Baseball League
NYCBL Overall Statistics (as of Aug 07, 2007)
(All games Sorted by Batting avg)

Player	AVG	GP-GS	AB	R	H	2B	3B	HR	RBI	TB
McIntyre, WY...........	.409	41-41	159	30	65	16	1	2	36	89
Riffee, SP.............	.373	22-19	67	18	25	4	0	0	5	29
Wolf, EP..............	.367	29-28	98	11	36	6	0	1	13	45
Witkowski, LF.........	.364	31-29	110	18	40	2	0	0	15	46
McGhee, AM...........	.350	38-38	157	28	55	8	2	0	15	67
Seaborn, AM..........	.350	39-35	140	25	49	11	0	6	27	78
Gaynor, EP...........	.350	41-41	163	30	57	13	2	1	25	77
Brewington, HD.......	.349	34-30	109	13	38	3	1	0	11	43
Parkinson, GR........	.348	22-18	66	11	23	2	0	0	6	25
Ferguson, BR.........	.338	36-36	148	26	50	8	0	2	24	64
DeGeorge, GF.........	.338	40-40	160	28	54	15	0	0	21	69
Sumner, BR...........	.337	33-27	95	17	32	2	2	2	17	44
Shaffer, GF..........	.333	37-37	144	21	48	9	3	1	21	66
Webb, SP.............	.329	38-37	155	32	51	7	1	3	22	69
Stokes, GR...........	.327	33-32	110	15	36	11	0	1	18	50

New York Collegiate Baseball League
NYCBL Overall Statistics (as of Aug 07, 2007)
(All games Sorted by Earned run avg)

Player	ERA	W-L	APP	GS	CG	SHO/CBO	SV	IP	H
Tenholder, HD...........	0.00	0-2	14	0	0	0/2	3	22.1	12
Dill, HD................	0.83	4-2	14	0	0	0/0	7	32.2	22
Bertuccini, GR..........	1.14	3-1	8	4	0	0/3	0	31.2	22
Lamm, SP................	1.19	2-1	9	4	0	0/0	1	30.1	15
Bellamy, GR.............	1.29	1-0	17	1	0	0/4	11	21.0	10
Wolf, EP................	1.31	3-0	8	8	0	0/2	0	48.0	35
Bowman, GR..............	1.32	3-1	9	5	1	1/1	0	41.0	31
Latta, GF...............	1.35	3-0	11	0	0	0/0	2	26.2	15
Gardner, WY.............	1.38	0-1	22	0	0	0/0	4	26.0	9
Mowdy, GR...............	1.46	6-0	13	5	0	0/1	0	49.1	26

Statistics courtesy of www.nycbl.com